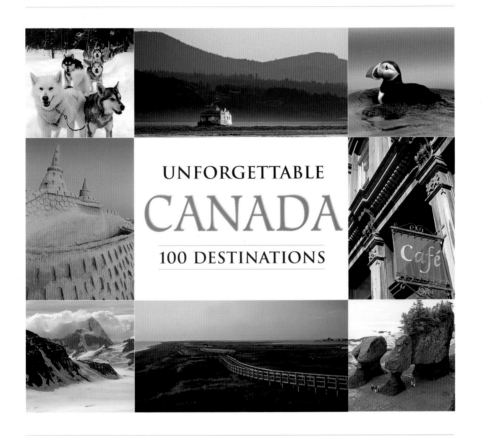

UNFORGETTABLE
CANADA
100 DESTINATIONS

UPDATED SECOND EDITION

UNFORGETTABLE

CANADA

100 DESTINATIONS

GEORGE FISCHER and NOEL HUDSON

The BOSTON
MILLS PRESS

For Marin, Walker and Tess
NH

For Debbie and Richard Gardos
GF

A BOSTON MILLS PRESS BOOK

Copyright © 2007 George Fischer and Noel Hudson

Second Edition, Second Printing, 2010

Published by Boston Mills Press, 2007
132 Main Street, Erin, Ontario N0B 1T0
Tel: 519-833-2407 Fax: 519-833-2195

In Canada:
Distributed by Firefly Books Ltd.
66 Leek Crescent
Richmond Hill, Ontario, Canada L4B 1H1

In the United States:
Distributed by Firefly Books (U.S.) Inc.
P.O. Box 1338, Ellicott Station
Buffalo, New York 14205

The publisher gratefully acknowledges the financial support for our publishing
program by the Government of Canada through the Canada Book Fund
as administered by the Department of Canadian Heritage.

Library and Archives Canada Cataloguing in Publication
Fischer, George, 1954-
Unforgettable Canada : 100 destinations / George Fischer and Noel Hudson.
Includes index.
ISBN-13: 978-1-55046-461-0
ISBN-10: 1-55046-461-2
1. Canada--Guidebooks.   2. Canada--Pictorial works.
I. Hudson, Noel, 1956- II. Title.
FC38.F49 2007   917.104'73   C2007-903153-6

Publisher Cataloging-in-Publication Data (U.S.)
Fischer, George.
Unforgettable Canada : 100 destinations / George Fischer and Noel Hudson
[288] p. : col. photos. ;   cm.
ISBN-13: 978-1-55046-461-0 (pbk.)
ISBN-10: 1-55046-461-2 (pbk.)
1. Canada — Description and travel — Guidebooks. 2. Canada — Guidebooks.
I. Hudson, Noel. II. Title.
917.104647 dc 22   F1017.F574 2007

Design by Gillian Stead
Scanning and color fidelity by Moveable Inc. (www.moveable.com)
Printed in China

100 DESTINATIONS

Dinosaur Provincial Park , AB

Little Doc Lake, NT

Arctic Toe Dip, Tuktoyaktuk, NT

Montreal Jazz Festival, QC

Cirque of the Unclimbables, NT

CN Tower, ON

Great Sand Hills, SK

Old Montreal, QC

Grand Manan, NB

Churchill's Polar Bears, MB

Masset Potlatch, BC

Cavendish
National Historic Site, PE

Salmon Fishing
in the Queen Charlottes, BC

PREFACE

Geographically speaking, Canada is enormous — the second-largest country in the world — so it stands to reason that, from sea to sea to sea, there are more than 100 destinations worth visiting. But we think this list is a great starting point for your journeys.

Photographer George Fischer and I reviewed dozens of "Top Destinations" lists from magazines, newspapers and travel-related websites. We also talked to people who have travelled extensively throughout Canada. We made working lists and revised them repeatedly. Our 100 destinations hovered around 130 for several weeks until the pressing need to make travel arrangements forced us to declare a final, definitive 100. This is our selection. We think it's a good one.

The 100 destinations appear in no particular order, destination #100 is no less worthy than destination #1, and we chose not to present them from east to west or west to east because we want to emphasize the incredible geographic diversity that Canada possesses. Some provinces and territories may be more spectacular than others due to their mountain ranges or coastal settings (or both!), but every province and territory has its own memorable sights.

We have attempted to be as factually accurate as possible. Most of the information in this book was checked and double-checked against standard reference works as well as the most current national, provincial and/or municipal tourism sources, national and provincial parks services websites, and so on. Additional historical and scientific information was obtained from a variety of sources; these were not always in precise agreement with each other. If the Top of the World Highway is 4 kilometres (2.5 mi) longer according to your odometer or your favourite birding reference claims that northern gannet chicks hatch in late June instead of early July, you may be correct. Please keep in mind that this is a book of proposed journeys and not a reference book.

We would also like to note that we didn't set out to promote Fairmont Hotels. It just happens that in the late 1800s and early 1900s, Canadian Pacific Railway president William Van Horne built some of the grandest luxury hotels in Canada at some of the most stunningly beautiful sites in Canada, and these hotels are now owned and operated by Fairmont — The Empress, Chateau Lake Louise, Banff Springs Hotel, Chateau Frontenac. In Van Horne's own words, "Since we can't export the scenery, we'll have to import the tourists."

As you enter these pages, we hope you'll allow yourself to be "imported" into Canada's unparalleled scenery, its magnificent parks and nature reserves, historic cities and charming villages, colourful festivals and uniquely Canadian activities.

We hope you like where this book takes you. ⌁

1

ICEBERG-WATCHING
∼ Newfoundland & Labrador

The eastern and northern coasts of Newfoundland and Labrador are the best places in the northern hemisphere to observe icebergs. Twillingate, Newfoundland, calls itself the Iceberg Capital of the World. Meanwhile, up the Great Northern Peninsula, the town of St. Anthony humbly claims to be the best place to watch icebergs. The fact is, there are many picturesque locations along Newfoundland and Labrador's coastlines that offer memorable iceberg-watching opportunities, and should you wish to take a closer look, no shortage of boats and tour guides to take you out to sea.

The best time to view icebergs is from April to July. The majority of these icebergs come from glaciers located along Greenland's western coast, though some are from eastern Canadian Arctic islands. In an average year, about 40,000 sizeable icebergs "calve off" in Greenland. Of those, only 1,500 or so reach Newfoundland waters before melting, and less than half that number make it as far south as St. John's. Numbers vary from year to year, and much about iceberg season depends on the weather three years previous, as it often takes an iceberg two or three years to make its way south to Newfoundland.

LEFT: You've probably used the expression "the tip of the iceberg." In order for an iceberg to float, approximately seven-eighths of its mass must be below water. This doesn't mean that the ice extends seven times as far below the water than it does above the water. It simply means that the portion of the iceberg that we cannot see is about seven times larger in mass than the "tip" that we can see.

RIGHT: Caution must be taken when approaching an iceberg. If it "calves off" or rolls, the resulting wave may be enough to capsize a boat. Underwater ice "rams" can pose an even greater threat. An iceberg's asymmetrical shape and uneven melting patterns cause it to be unpredictable. These pristine, silent, behemoth bergs may fracture, calve or roll over completely without warning.

RIGHT and BELOW: Iceberg ice is pure, fresh water and thus is a valuable commodity as bottled drinking water and as a component in select vodkas and other products. The glacial ice is formed from thousands of years of compacted snow. While the layers of ice may contain trace levels of airborne dust or ash from volcanic eruptions thousands of years ago, pollutant levels are almost zero.

The icebergs that reach Newfoundland's east coast often spend a year or more passing through the Davis Strait before entering the frigid Labrador Current. Once they enter the Current, they are pushed southward through Flemish Pass and down the eastern side of the Grand Banks.

Icebergs float because the density of freshwater ice is less than that of seawater. The average weight of an iceberg found along the Grand Banks is between 100,000 and 200,000 tons, but they can weigh several million tons and easily tower 20 storeys or more above the waterline.

Icebergs tend to travel at less than one kilometre per hour, though they can reach speeds of up to almost four kilometres per hour, depending on size and current. Because they move so slowly, they rarely travel in a straight line but rather meander subject to the strength of cross currents.

The ocean corridor from northern Labrador to the southern Grand Banks has long been known as Iceberg Alley. Hundreds upon hundreds of ships have met their icy end in these waters. Underwater archaeologists have found shipwrecks dating back to 1550–1600, when this region was considered the whaling capital of the world, supplying Europe with whale oil for lamps, heating fuel and for use in the manufacture of wool, leather and soap.

Glaciers consist of ice formed by annual snowfalls compacting layer upon layer over thousands of years. As floating pieces of glaciers, icebergs consist of the same ancient ice. Less dense ice contains air bubbles, and it is the light-reflecting quality of these air bubbles that give most icebergs their white appearance. Sections of icebergs with few or no air bubbles reflect light differently and appear blue.

In most cases modern ships can spot icebergs in shipping lanes and make their way safely around them, but stationary offshore oil platforms occasionally find themselves positioned precariously in an iceberg's path. This has led to advanced iceberg-detection methods and an iceberg-towing industry. Imagine listing your occupation as "Iceberg Mover" on your tax forms.

2 DEMPSTER HIGHWAY
~ Yukon / Northwest Territories

The Dempster Highway is Canada's most northerly highway, the only highway in the western hemisphere to cross the Arctic Circle. It traverses vast stretches of tundra, winds its way through deep canyons and past some of Canada's highest waterfalls, crosses the Continental Divide three times, and eventually passes through the Richardson Mountains, the northernmost extent of the Rockies, and onto the Mackenzie River delta.

When most of us think of "highway," we envision a well-maintained four-lane blacktop with nice stripes down the middle to guide us. The Dempster is 740 kilometres (460 mi) of groomed gravel. It runs from a junction 40 kilometres (25 mi) east of Dawson City to Inuvik, in the Northwest Territories. In winter, it extends via ice road to Tuktoyaktuk, on the Beaufort Sea.

The Dempster Highway is named for Inspector William Dempster of the Royal Canadian Mounted Police. Dempster came to the Yukon during the Klondike Gold Rush of 1898. In winter he famously patrolled a route from Dawson City all the way to Fort McPherson by dogsled, in temperatures often reaching -40 degrees (many years before the calculation of wind-chill factors). This feat of cold, hard endurance rightly earned him the nickname "Iron Man of the Trail." Inspector Dempster retired to far more temperate Vancouver in 1934.

The drive is long, bumpy and features some of the most pristine wilderness scenery on Earth.

While most of the road is in commendable shape, the potholes are large and the ubiquitous sharp-edged shale can rapidly wear down tires and turn your car's paint job into abstract art. It's a good idea to hire a rental car or borrow one from someone whose friendship you no longer value. Of course, there's always the way of two wheels. (Bring extra tires.)

ABOVE: To prevent the permafrost layer from thawing, the highway is built atop an insulating gravel cushion ranging 1.5 to 2.5 metres (5 to 8 ft) thick. Without that cushion, the permafrost would melt and the road would sink.

Dempster's namesake highway officially opened in 1979 and roughly follows the trail he patrolled as a young RCMP officer. He is said to have been shown the trail by the region's Gwich'in people, whose ancestors used it as a trade route between the Peel and Yukon river systems for hundreds of years.

The Canadian government declared their intention to build the highway in 1958. Oil and gas exploration was booming along the Mackenzie delta, and the proposed road would serve as an overland supply route to fuel-hungry cities in the south. But high construction costs and squabbles between federal and provincial governments made for slow progress, and by 1961 road construction had come to a standstill.

ABOVE: When people talk about travelling to the ends of the earth, this must be what they mean. It's possible to drive through mountains and valleys for hours without seeing another human being. Most visitors are surprised to find this extreme escape from civilization strangely comforting.

When U.S. companies announced the discovery of massive oil and gas reserves in Alaska in 1968, proposed pipeline routes and concern over sovereignty issues resurrected the project. The 1970s saw its completion.

Two major bridges carry motorists over the Ogilvie and Eagle rivers, and ferries take aboard cars at the Peel River crossing near Fort McPherson and the Arctic Red River crossing near Tsiigehtchic. Ferries are operational from late May or early June until October, with ice bridges providing passage from December to March, more or less. Everything up here depends on weather conditions, so it's best to check the local and regional weather often if you're travelling any time other than summer.

In early July each year, the Richardson Mountains become home to the migrating Porcupine caribou herd, one of the largest herds of barren-ground caribou in the world, thought to number approximately 130,000. Other resident wildlife includes Dall's sheep, muskoxen, moose, grizzlies, black bear, Arctic wolves and rare gyrfalcons. The Mackenzie Valley is a migratory corridor for millions of waterfowl on their way to Arctic breeding grounds. Among the most remarkable of these species is the sandhill crane, which stand about 1.2 metres (4 ft) tall and have wingspans of more than 2 metres (6.5 ft). During migration, several thousand may travel in a single flock.

It takes 14 hours or so to drive the Dempster in good weather, but take your time and stop frequently. In this case, the journey *is* the destination. ⌁

RIGHT: Seasonally colourful foxtail barley (also called squirreltail) can be seen along many stretches of the Dempster. While quite at home in the North's dry meadows, it is not an indigenous plant. It is thought to have arrived in the North as a result of being shipped from Montreal in straw used to pack freighter canoes destined for Hudson's Bay Company outposts.

ABOVE: Dall's sheep are well adapted to mountain living, where grasses and other low-growing plants provide abundant food. They have keen eyesight and their cloven, concave hooves make them agile on rocky slopes. They inhabit the Richardson and Mackenzie mountains of the Western Arctic.

3 PARKSVILLE BEACH FESTIVAL

~ British Columbia

E ach August, as part of its popular Beach Festival, the small Vancouver Island community of Parksville hosts the Canadian Open Sand Sculpting Competition and Exhibition.

The Oceanside region on Vancouver Island's sheltered central east coast is home to three of the Pacific Northwest's best beaches: Rathtrevor Beach, located at the south end of Parksville; Parksville Community Beach; and Qualicum Beach, just a few kilometres up scenic Oceanside Route 19A from Parksville. Each beach has its own personality, but all three share long stretches of sand and the warmest ocean current north of Big Sur, California.

Parksville Community Beach stretches some 5 kilometres (3 mi) along Parksville Bay, which itself becomes one large beach when the tide goes out. And it's here that the Parksville Beach Festival holds its annual sandcastle competition, complete with a children's contest that draws over 1,000 entries each year.

The North American Bus Association, which reviews travel destinations, made the Parksville Beach Festival one of its top 100 events for 2006. The festival was even mentioned on the *Oprah Winfrey Show* as a "must see" event on Vancouver Island.

People come from all over the world to marvel at these amazing works of art and engineering. The 2005 competition saw visitors from 73 countries in attendance, including guests from every Canadian province and territory and all 50 American states.

The sculpture competition's total prize money is currently $25,000, with the first-place solo category winner earning $3,100 and the first-place team category winners earning $3,500. Cash awards are given for other rankings, from second- to fifth-place winners, in each category.

Lasting 23 days in August, the event is completely organized and run by community volunteer groups and is the largest, longest-running event on Vancouver Island. The sand-sculpting competition attracts artists from around the globe. The competition lasts for 23 hours, spread over three days. The sculptures remain in place for three weeks following the competition, and admission is by donation.

Each solo artist gets a 1.4-square-metre (15 sq ft) plot and 10 tons of clean sand, and each team gets a 2.8-square-metre (30 sq ft) plot and 20 tons of sand. Rules stipulate that contestants must use all of their allotted sand.

The competition was deemed a great success by local media when 100 people attended the first "B.C. Open" sand-sculpting event in 1982. Known today as the Canadian Open Sand Sculpting Competition, the event has evolved into a world-class challenge that attracts over 70,000 visitors.

4

Le PAYS de la SAGOUINE
~ New Brunswick

The village of Le Pays de la Sagouine is a working Acadian village lifted from the pages of writer Antonine Maillet's 1971 book *La Sagouine* (translated into English in 1979). The name of the village translates as "the land of the poor woman who scrubs floors." According to Maillet, the reference is to the women who took the train into Moncton every day to clean offices and homes during the 1930s.

Despite that dreary reference, the main character in Maillet's book, a 72-year-old cleaning woman, is fiery and full of wisdom and humour. Maillet dominated contemporary Acadian literature, winning many awards for her work. The publication of *La Sagouine* coincided with a revival of Acadian culture in Canada, lending a literary voice to an often overlooked people and their history.

. . . and no shortage of authentic Acadian food and drink.

Le Pays de la Sagouine is reached via a wooden footbridge. Here, an Acadian fishing village from the 1930s is recreated from local memory and from the novels and plays of writer Antonine Maillet.

ABOVE: This authentically recreated village comes alive with theatre, music, comedy and dance each summer and allows visitors to discover true Acadian culture. For an even more lively time, stop for a drink in the village's own *Bootleggeux*.

It is the lively depiction of this history and culture, every day, all summer long, which attracts thousands of visitors to Le Pays de la Sagouine each year. Acadian music can be heard no matter where you go on the small island, and a comedy troupe performs skits by Maillet. There are artists and dancers, storytellers and clairvoyants, and no shortage of authentic Acadian food and drink.

The many colourful residents of Le Pays de la Sagouine demonstrate how Acadian joie de vivre has triumphed over hard times for centuries. ◠

LEFT: Le Pays de la Sagouine translates as "the land of the poor woman who scrubs floors." According to author Antonine Maillet, the reference is to the Acadian women who took the train to Moncton every day to clean.

5

NORTH of SUPERIOR

~ Ontario

Here's an interesting statistic: Northern Ontario makes up 85 percent of Ontario's landmass, while Southern Ontario has 94 percent of the province's population. The majority of that population has never been to Lake Superior.

Being the largest of the Great Lakes, it's not an easy geographic feature to overlook. It has the largest surface area of any freshwater lake in the world. It stretches approximately 560 kilometres (350 mi) from west to east, and 255 kilometres (160 mi) north to south. Often referred to as an inland sea, Superior is vast and, for the most part, wild.

Some of Lake Superior's most beautiful scenery can be found along its northern shores: cliff-top vistas, rugged bluffs, smooth-stoned beaches, and emerald archipelagos. A great place to start is Ontario's Pukaskwa National Park. Located about halfway between Sault Ste. Marie and Thunder Bay, it encompasses 1880 square kilometres (725 sq mi) of rugged shoreline, ancient rock and pristine forest. Founded in 1978, Pukaskwa protects and preserves largely unaltered stretches of the Central Boreal Uplands and the northern Great Lakes coast.

BELOW: Eastern white pine can live 500 years and attain a height of 50 metres (165 ft), given optimum growing conditions. This magnificent feathery-limbed species is Ontario's official tree.

ABOVE: During the first half of the twentieth century, timber companies logged the boreal forest of Lake Superior's north shore for pulpwood and paper. The trees, cut in early winter, were floated down the rivers in spring and collected in bays by huge free-floating booms. A woody carpet of sunken logs collected on the lake bottom in places like McGreevy Harbour in the Slate Islands.

BELOW: Sunset at Tugboat Channel, Gargantua, Lake Superior Provincial Park.

Or pick a provincial park as your destination — Neys, Rainbow Falls, Sleeping Giant, Kakabeka, Ouimet Canyon and others provide a gateway to an unforgettable Superior experience.

The photographs for this chapter were provided by Gary and Joanie McGuffin, who live in the Algoma Highlands overlooking Lake Superior. The McGuffins are founders of the Lake Superior Conservancy and Watershed Council, an international non-profit organization dedicated to preserving the Lake Superior watershed. ⌁

6

DINOSAUR PROVINCIAL PARK & BADLANDS
~ Alberta

Located in the heart of the Alberta badlands, roughly two hours east of Calgary, Dinosaur Provincial Park contains some of the world's most important fossil discoveries from the Mesozoic Era, 245 to 65 million years ago, commonly known as the "Age of Reptiles." More than 300 dinosaur skeletons have been unearthed in the park, which was designated a UNESCO World Heritage Site in 1979. These finds include well-preserved remains of about 35 dinosaur species from around 75 million years ago.

At that time in geological history, this area was a subtropical lowland plain at the edge of a vast shallow sea that extended from southeastern Alberta to the Gulf of Mexico. When animals died on the mudflats, they were gradually covered by layer upon layer of sediment, which over time compressed and, compounded by the effects of mineralization, produced a large number of remarkably intact fossil remains. Some of the best of these finds are now held in the collection of the Royal Tyrell Museum of Paleontology, 6 kilometres (4 mi) northwest of Drumheller. The museum is named for geologist Joseph Burr Tyrell, who discovered the first Albertosaurus skull in these badlands in 1884.

The rugged Drumheller Valley badlands feature such dramatic erosion formations as buttes, canyons, coulees, gullies, glacial erratics, freestanding boulders and sink holes, but by far the most striking features are the hoodoos.

This was a hub of activity during the age of reptiles.

LEFT: The prairie landscape takes a sudden turn for the surreal when it drops abruptly into the badlands. Here, rock formations have been eroded by glaciers, wind and water over thousands of years to produce otherworldly shapes. During the Age of Reptiles, this region was on the northern edge of a great inland sea that extended as far south as the Gulf of Mexico.

RIGHT: Designated a UNESCO World Heritage Site, the park is of great international paleontological significance. Tens of thousands of fossil specimens have been collected, including some of the world's best representations of dinosaurs from the Late Cretaceous Period. This life-size replica assures visitors that they've come to the right place.

First Nations people first discovered animal fossils in this area. They believed them to have been gigantic ancestors of the bison. The hard-capped sandstone formations that they called hoodoos were thought to be the protectors of the bison and ancient animals' spirits.

RIGHT: French-Canadian explorers François and Louis Joseph de la Verendrye described this arid land, unsuitable to farming, as "les mauvaises terres" (literally "bad lands"). While these lands were indeed bad for growing crops, they proved themselves rich in coal and fossils. The Sioux people of what is now North Dakota are said to have called their similar landscape "Mako Sika" ("lands bad").

Hoodoos are vertical structures of soft sandstone capped with harder sandstone. Wind and water wear away the standing pillars at a much faster rate than their cap-rocks, creating strange totem-like figures.

You'll also notice the surrounding slopes are made up of multicoloured layers of exposed rock. Except for the soft top layer of coarse soil, these layers date back 65 to 75 million years to a time just before extinction of the dinosaurs. Layers from more recent time periods have been eroded by weather and water or scraped away by glacial action.

Though the landscape appears ancient, it looked nothing like this when the dinosaurs lived here 230 million to 65 million years ago. At that time, it was a series of deltas and flood plains stretching east into the warm, shallow sea that covered much of inland North America. ∽

LEFT: Since 1985, many of the spectacular finds from Dinosaur Provincial Park have been housed at the Royal Tyrell Museum of Paleontology. Other dinosaur skeletons from the park are featured in museum collections in 30 cities around the globe.

7

KAYAKING
with KILLER WHALES
∼ British Columbia

LEFT: Sea-kayaking is a great way to travel these protected waters. There is nothing quite like being at water level when an orca breaches nearby. Be sure to listen carefully. Orcas communicate with each other by a complex range of clicks, whistles and scream-like pulses.

Johnstone Strait, off the east coast of Vancouver Island, is home to approximately 200 orcas, the largest resident pod of killer whales in the world. There is no better place to see these beautiful creatures.

Gouged deep and narrow by ice-age glaciers, Johnstone Strait runs from approximately Telegraph Cove in the north to Rock Bay in the south. Pods of orcas come to these waters each summer for the annual salmon runs that begin in late June. Orcas are efficient hunters and eat a diverse diet of fish, squid, octopi, seals, sharks, turtles and seabirds, as well as other whale species. Members of a pod frequently cooperate in hunts, and an average-sized orca will eat 250 kilograms (550 lbs) of food a day.

BELOW: Orcas grow to be about 8 to 10 metres long (27-33 ft) and can weigh more than 5 metric tons (12,000 lbs). Male orcas have a life expectancy of 50 to 60 years, while females often live to 90 years.

ABOVE: Many towns along the island's east coast offer whale-watching excursions by kayak or cruise, but Telegraph Cove is where whale-watching on the strait really begins. This tiny community, with its full-time population of only 20 people, is nestled into some of the last pristine coastline on the continent.

Though whale-watching tours are readily available, perhaps the most exciting way to approach killer whales is quietly aboard a sea kayak. Sea-kayaking provides a thrilling nearness to the ocean and its creatures that cannot be duplicated by travel in larger vessels.

Robson Bight Ecological Reserve, about 20 kilometres (12 mi) south of Telegraph Cove, offers orca-watchers the best chance they'll ever have to see the top of the ocean food chain.

Minke, humpback and grey whales, white-sided dolphins, porpoises, harbour seals and sea lions are among the other marine animals seen regularly in the Johnstone Strait area. ~

LEFT: Picturesque Telegraph Cove is built on stilts and linked by a wooden boardwalk. Many of this tiny sawmill and cannery community's original buildings still stand.

8

OLD QUEBEC CITY
~ Quebec

Quebec is the only remaining fortified city in North America. An estimated six million people a year visit the city's ramparts and bastions, well-preserved architectural evidence of over three centuries of its military past. It is these fortifications and the history behind them that brought about the district's designation as a UNESCO World Heritage Site in 1985.

About half the buildings in Quebec's historic district were built before 1850, with some of the district's architecture dating back to the days of New France. Though Quebec City has grown into a modern urban centre in many respects, the many heritage buildings at its core give it an Old World feel. It is the only walled city on the continent and the only city to have retained almost all of its historic fortifications.

Quebec City is home to over two dozen designated historic sites.

Home to the first settlers of New France, Lower Town encompasses the old port district and is reached from Upper Town via a steep, winding street called Côte de la Montagne and the appropriately named Escalier Casse-Cou (Breakneck Stairs). Lower Town is the nucleus from which Quebec grew.

Old Quebec City covers about 135 hectares (334 acres), about five percent of the total city. It was in the Lower Town (Basse-Ville) section that Samuel de Champlain took up residence in 1608. In 1688 Place Royale was created as a cobbled market square and a place for public meetings, on the former site of Champlain's garden. Notre-Dame-des-Victoires church, also built in 1688, occupies the site of Champlain's original home. Directly south from the square is Rue du Petit-Champlain, Quebec's oldest street and North America's oldest commercial thoroughfare. ～

BELOW: Many calèche companies provide sleigh-ride tours in the winter months. Bundle up, toss a blanket over your knee and pretend you're in a Krieghoff painting.

LEFT: Fairmont Le Chateau Frontenac is located on Cape Diamond bluff, high above the St. Lawrence River, in the heart of Old Quebec. Opened in 1893, it is one the most photographed buildings in North America.

The Chateau Frontenac was designed by architect Bruce Price for the Canadian Pacific Railway, who thought a series of chateau-style hotels might bolster luxury tourism along its lines. The Frontenac is named for Louis de Buade, Count of Frontenac, governor of New France in the late 1600s.

9

AUYUITTUQ NATIONAL PARK
∼ Nunavut

Auyuittuq National Park Reserve is located on Baffin Island's Cumberland Peninsula. Over three quarters of the park is situated inside the Arctic Circle. *Auyuittuq* is an Inuktitut word meaning "the land that never melts."

Formed by ancient episodes of glacial action, the park features some of the highest peaks on the Canadian Shield, as well as the Penny Ice Cap, coastal fiords and the seasonally hike-able Akshayuk Pass, a natural corridor used by Inuit for thousands of years. Modern Inuit residents trace their lineage back to the Thule people, who reached the eastern Arctic in the eleventh century, but there is evidence in the park of Dorset culture dating back as much as 3,000 years.

RIGHT: Formerly known as Pangnirtung Pass, Akshayuk Pass offers a spectacular 100-kilometre (62 mi) hike. For the more moderately ambitious, there is a 20-kilometre (12 mi) hike from the south of the park to Summit Lake.

BELOW: Summit Lake marks the highest point in Akshayuk Pass. This large lake was formed by glacial meltwaters in an end moraine. Water from this lake flows both north and south, dropping 500 metres (1,640 ft) before reaching the Arctic Ocean.

ABOVE: The cylindrical towers of Mount Asgard rise from amidst surrounding Turner and Highway glaciers. These glaciers creep in imperceptibly slow motion toward the valley floor.

The oldest rock on the Cumberland Peninsula dates back 2.8 billion years. It became exposed around 60 million years ago when the peninsula was uplifted as continental drift caused Baffin Island to break off from Greenland.

This is a land of steep rock faces, boulder fields, glaciers, icefields and high tundra. The resulting shortage of vegetation makes wildlife sightings scarce, but hikers may occasionally sight barren-ground caribou, Arctic hare, Arctic fox, ermine and the park's two species of lemming. More plentiful numbers of marine mammals occur in coastal fiords along Davis Strait, including ringed seal, bearded seal, narwhal, beluga whale, orca and polar bear.

Break-up usually occurs toward the end of June, and a new layer of snow often begins to accumulate in September, so plan your visit accordingly.

RIGHT: The imaginary line known as the Arctic Circle is marked by a monument along the trail. At any point along the Circle, there are 24 hours of daylight on June 21 and 24 hours of darkness on December 21. The park remains in near-constant darkness between October and February.

10

CAPE SPEAR NATIONAL HISTORIC SITE
∾ Newfoundland & Labrador

Cape Spear is the most easterly point of land in North America. Rising 75 metres (246 ft) above sealevel and jutting almost defiantly into the waves of the cold Atlantic, this was the "Land ho!" for many early transatlantic seamen. It also claimed many lives as, shrouded in fog and lashed by vicious storms, it could just as easily bring a ship crashing ashore.

The first Cape Spear lighthouse beamed its warning light out to sea in 1836. As technology advanced, the light was upgraded many times. The last of the lights in the old Cape Spear lighthouse was a glass dioptric system installed in 1912. That dioptric system was moved to a new light tower, not far from the original lighthouse, in 1955. The present lighthouse has been restored to its original appearance and is the most recognized aspect of Cape Spear National Historic Site.

The oldest surviving lighthouse in Newfoundland and Labrador, Cape Spear lighthouse has been restored to its original appearance and refurnished as a circa-1839 lightkeeper's residence.

ABOVE: St. John's builders Nicholas Croke and William Parker began work on the lighthouse in 1834 or early in 1835, and the light was operational by September 1836. The original Cape Spear lighthouse was framed as a two-storey square building with the light tower at its centre.

The site also contains bunkers and gun barrels from a Second World War coastal defense battery intended to protect St. John's harbour from enemy submarines. Troops were stationed here from 1941 until the end of hostilities in 1945.

Today, Cape Spear serves as a great location from which to watch for whales, dolphins, porpoises, seals, seabirds, icebergs and ship traffic into and out of St. John's harbour. ◁

RIGHT and OPPOSITE: For many early transatlantic mariners, this rugged coastline was the first sight of land after a long voyage. The Portuguese called it "Cabo da Esperança," which means "cape of hope." In French it was "Cap d'Espoir." The English translated by sound rather than meaning, and thus we have "Cape Spear."

11

LITTLE DOCTOR LAKE
～ Northwest Territories

LEFT: Little Doctor Lake's shape has been likened to "a blunt-tipped arrowhead shot into the Nahanni Range." The steep rockface through which it plunges is known as the Gap.

L ittle Doctor Lake is one of Canada's secret places, tucked away in the wild expanse of the Northwest Territories, overshadowed by neighbouring Nahanni National Park.

When northern pioneers and local legends Gus and Mary Kraus found their Nahanni cabin and namesake Kraus Hotsprings incorporated into the park, this is where they moved. It is a bit of heaven on Earth.

According to the Krauses, Little Doctor was named for a Dene medicine man. Their lodge is now owned and operated by Ted Grant, who also operates Simpson Air, the oldest established air charter company in the Nahanni–Ram Plateau region. Grant found himself stationed in Fort Simpson as a member of the RCMP in the mid-1970s. Overwhelmed by the beauty of this pristine northern wilderness, he decided to stay. You'll want to, too. ～

BELOW: Ted Grant's Simpson Air flies direct to Little Doctor Lake from Fort Simpson. Passengers have included wildlife artist Robert Bateman, adventure clothier Alex Tilley, professional sports figures, statesmen and even Britain's Prince Andrew.

12 THOUSAND ISLANDS

~ Ontario

While making his way through the Thousand Islands region in 1615, French explorer Samuel de Champlain wrote in his journal, "The whole country is very beautiful and attractive. Along the riverbank, it seemed as if the trees had been planted for pleasure."

The picturesque Thousand Islands actually number closer to 2,000. They rise in rocky outcrops of all shapes and sizes for about 96 kilometres (60 mi), from the western head of the St. Lawrence River into eastern Lake Ontario. Don't be fooled by the presence of modern watercraft, these islands have ancient origins. The surrounding pink granite was thrust up from deep in the earth hundreds of millions of years ago. The youngest rock in the region is the exposed limestone, which was laid down a mere 450 million years ago.

This is a place where scenery and history compete for a visitor's attention. The international border between Canada and the United States weaves its way erratically through the islands as a result of many decades of claims and negotiations — even battles. Many of the area's first settlers were United Empire Loyalists who moved north following the American War of Independence. There were constant skirmishes across the river during the War of 1812, and some islands still bear the names of British warships (Deathdealer, Bloodletter, Scorpion) and admirals (Lindsey, Melville). Other islands were named for their more agrarian purposes (Turnip, Corn, Potato, Sheep, Hog). Everywhere you turn in the Thousand Islands, history is in evidence.

Don't be afraid to be a tourist. Scenic boat tours through the Thousand Islands have been plying these waters since the late 1800s. ❧

ABOVE: The Thousand Islands are really closer to 2,000 islands, a number determined using the criteria that a "countable" island must remain above water level all 365 days per year and must support at least one tree or shrub. The islands are located where part of the massive Canadian Shield rock formation trails south across the St. Lawrence to connect with the Adirondack Mountain chain.

LEFT: One of the major attractions in the Thousand Islands is Boldt Castle on Heart Island. The castle was to be a tribute to Waldorf Astoria owner George Boldt's love for his wife, Louise. Work commenced in 1900 on a planned 11 buildings, including extensive boathouses for a fleet of yachts, launches and steamboats. When Louise died suddenly and mysteriously in January 1904, George halted construction, left the islands and never returned. Visitors from all over the world make romantic pilgrimages to Boldt Castle.

RIGHT: The Thousand Islands are a boater's paradise. Antique mahogany launches join sailboats, yachts, speedboats, tour boats, fishing boats, steamboats, houseboats, kayaks and canoes in this place where pirates and bootleggers once evaded the lawmen from both the U.S. and Canada.

HISTORIC LUNENBURG
⁓ Nova Scotia

Established in 1753, the south-coast Nova Scotia town of Lunenburg is the best surviving example of a planned British colonial settlement in North America. As such, it has been designated as a UNESCO World Heritage Site.

For well over 250 years Lunenburg has retained its original rectangular grid layout of streets, as drafted by town planners in "the home country," and of the 400 or so major buildings in Lunenburg's Old Town section, almost two thirds date back to the eighteenth and nineteenth centuries. Most are constructed entirely of wood and many have been painted vibrant colours.

Lunenburg is home to the Fisheries Museum of the Atlantic and home port of the tall ship *Bluenose II*, a replica of the original *Bluenose*.

RIGHT: Residents have safeguarded Lunenburg's historic importance by preserving much of its original wooden architecture.

ABOVE: Lunenburg has been a strong and vital community for more than 250 years, with an economy based on fishing, shipbuilding, ocean-based trade and, in more recent decades, tourism.

Colonial policy dictated that a pre-designed model-town plan be applied to all new British settlements. Of course, these models completely disregarded local topography, and most North American cities and towns have long since departed from their original grids. But Lunenburg has benefitted from its historical links. Thousands of visitors arrive each summer to experience the community's maritime history and charm. ◿

LEFT: Lunenburg is home to the Fisheries Museum of the Atlantic and home port of the tall ship *Bluenose II*, a replica of the original *Bluenose*. Visiting tall ships such as the *Hector*, seen here, often frequent the town's historic harbour.

14 WORLD'S TALLEST TOTEM POLE
~ British Columbia

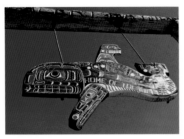

The world's tallest totem pole is located on the outskirts of the Nimpkish Reserve at Alert Bay, on the northern end of Cormorant Island. It reaches skyward to a height of almost 53 metres (173 ft). The thirteen main figures carved on this pole represent tribes of the Kwakwaka'wakw nation. A collection of traditional memorial poles can be seen nearby at the Alert Bay's Nimpkish (or Namgis) burial grounds, but please respect the sacred nature of these grounds and view them from the road.

The U'mista Cultural Centre at Alert Bay houses one of the world's finest collections of artifacts and carved masks related to the potlatch ceremony. In 1884 the Dominion government outlawed the potlatch ceremonies of the Kwakwaka'wakw people. Traditionally held to mark births, marriages and deaths, these ceremonies continued in secret, but in 1921 forty-five people were

The world's tallest totem pole is found on the outskirts of the Nimpkish Reserve at Alert Bay. It stands nearly 53 metres (173 ft) high and was built in two parts, one of 51 metres (168 ft), the other 1.5 metres (5 ft). The main figures carved on this pole represent tribes of the Kwakwaka'wakw nation.

ABOVE: lert Bay is located on crescent-shaped Cormorant Island, just off the northeast coast of Vancouver Island, approximately 330 kilometres (180 mi) by water from mainland Vancouver. It is located in the waters of British Columbia's beautiful Inside Passage and can be reached by taking a 40-minute ferry ride from Port McNeill.

Alert Bay is the oldest community on the north end of Vancouver Island.

RIGHT: Memorial totem poles marking some of the graves in these century-old burial grounds commemorate deceased members of the Nimpkish (or Namgis) band. Many figures carved on these poles represent family crests.

charged with holding a potlatch on Village Island. Ceremonial regalia were subsequently confiscated and distributed to museums or sold to private collectors across North America. While many of these artifacts have been returned in recent years, the process is ongoing.

The oldest community on the north end of Vancouver Island, Alert Bay has become well known for the powerful resurgence of its Native culture and possesses some of the region's finest historical and cultural artifacts, visual art and totem poles. The region also offers top-notch kayaking and whale-watching opportunities and some of the best saltwater fishing in British Columbia. ⌇

15 LAND of LIVING SKIES
～ Saskatchewan

Few people plan holiday visits to the Canadian prairies for the scenery, but anyone who has witnessed the panoramic light show of a prairie sunset or watched a thunderstorm approach at its leisure over distant fields knows the grandeur of the great, wide-open Saskatchewan sky. Saskatchewan's license plates feature the words "Land of Living Skies," and the province's citizens have every right to that boast.

ABOVE: An area of about 40,500 hectares (100,000 acres) south of Lake Manitou has been set aside as a protected habitat for migrating birds. Manitou Lake is considered an important stopover for migratory shorebirds and home to endangered species such as the piping plover

BELOW: Forget widescreen TV, Saskatchewan offers nature in all its panoramic splendour. Prairie sunsets are unrivalled.

ABOVE: One of the most dramatic pairings of land and sky occurs when canola fields are in bloom. Canola is Saskatchewan's second most important crop, after wheat.

The sky is worth watching for another reason. The province is considered to be the home, a key migratory stop or a breeding ground for over 350 bird species. Saskatchewan hosts over 25 percent of the continent's waterfowl, and swans and sandhill cranes congregate here by the millions each summer. Saskatchewan is also one of the best places to view whooping cranes, which can feed here for over a month before resuming migration. ∾

LEFT: The continent's oldest bird sanctuary, at Last Mountain Lake, between Regina and Saskatoon, was established in 1887. Every year, hundreds of thousands of waterfowl congregate here. It is an important breeding ground for over 100 individual species.

16

TUKTOYAKTUK, and PINGOS
∼ Northwest Territories

LEFT: The Arctic Toe Dip is a traditional rite of passage for travellers who reach the Arctic Ocean. These three beautiful Inuvialuit girls demonstrate how it's done.

Tuktoyaktuk is Canada's Timbuktu, an almost imaginary place at the distant edge of our geographical realm. Few Canadians have made their way this far north and few could locate it on a map, but most know the name of this hamlet of under 1,000 residents. It's part of our cultural vocabulary. If someone tells us, "I might as well have gone to Tuktoyaktuk," we know they travelled an extraordinary distance.

Tuktoyaktuk does exist. It is located on the Beaufort Sea, near the mouth of the Mackenzie River, about 150 kilometres (95 mi) north of Inuvik. It is accessible by air and seasonally by boat or ice road.

BELOW: The Inuvialuit, descendants of the Thule people who arrived here more than 1,000 years ago, hunted abundant herds of caribou. Tuktoyaktuk is said to be the anglicized spelling of Tuktuujaqrtuuq, which means "it looks like caribou." Many locals still rely on hunting, fishing and trapping.

Pingos rise up from the Arctic tundra like strange miniature volcanoes. A pingo is a hill with a core of ice and an outer layer of permafrost. They range from a few metres to as much as 70 metres (230 ft) in height. The Tuktoyaktuk region has the world's greatest concentration of pingos, over 1,300, and some of the largest. The 1,000-year-old Ibyuk Pingo stands 50 metres (164 ft) high and is the largest in Canada.

ABOVE: Radio station CFCT in Tuktoyaktuk made the *New York Times* on May 3, 1981, when the financially troubled station was reported as "being rescued from bankruptcy with the help of Radio Moscow…and the resulting controversy is sparking some hot tempers on both sides of the polar icecap."

Tuktoyaktuk is commonly referred to as Tuk, though any southerner who complains about trying to pronounce Tuktoyaktuk should know that it was once a prime site for hunting *tuku* (caribou) and was called Tuktuuyaqtuumukkabsi or Tuktuujaqrtuuq ("it looks like caribou") by the Inuvialuit, the Inuit of the western Arctic.

Tuk's original inhabitants, the Kittegaryumiut Inuit, survived by hunting whales until the people fell victim to a series of epidemics around the beginning of the twentieth century. A port community was established here in 1934, and the modern village of Tuktoyaktuk was incorporated in 1970.

At 69° 26′ 20″ North latitude, Tuktoyaktuk is a great place to view the Northern Lights.

17

LAKE LOUISE
~ Alberta

Tom Wilson was a packhorse owner working for the Canadian Pacific Railway when he became the first European to set eyes on the spectacular site now known as Lake Louise. It was 1882, and his Stoney guide led him to the place the Stoney people called "Lake of Little Fishes." Wilson is said to have declared the combination of glacier, snow-capped peaks and turquoise lake "a matchless scene." Each year, a million or so visitors agree.

Wilson took it upon himself to name the lake Emerald Lake, though its name was soon entered into official record as Lake Louise, for Queen Victoria's fourth daughter, Princess Louise Caroline Alberta, wife of Sir John Campbell, Governor General of Canada from 1878 to 1883.

BELOW: The lake's striking colour is due to the rock flour suspended in its waters. Rock flour is created through the process of glacial erosion. Glaciers drag across bedrock, creating clay-like grey-white particles the consistency of flour. These particles are then flushed into the lake.

ABOVE: The Fairmont Chateau Lake Louise is approximately two hours west of Calgary by car. It stands atop the huge glacial moraine that dams the lake.

Lake Louise is actually more turquoise than emerald, particularly in summer, when the sun's warm rays are refracted by fine rock particles suspended in the water.

The Canadian Pacific Railway constructed a log cabin here in 1890, but by 1900 the cabin had been replaced by the first Chateau Lake Louise, with accommodations for 200 guests. Perched majestically atop the glacial moraine that dams the lake, today's Chateau has been expanded over the years and can now house approximately 1,100 guests.

While the lake may be at its most photogenic in summer, winter visitors come to ski the area's 1700 hectares (4,200 acres) of mountain powder. Whatever the season, the combination of scenic grandeur and architectural elegance make Lake Louise an unforgettable destination. ∽

RIGHT: Lake Louise's north-shore trail winds past 90-metre (300 ft) cliffs, then leads hikers up through a forest and across avalanche slopes until six glaciers come into view. The path eventually reaches a teahouse built in 1924

18

L'ANSE aux MEADOWS NATIONAL HISTORIC SITE
∼ Newfoundland & Labrador

L'Anse aux Meadows is one of the most important archaeological sites in North America. There is evidence that Native peoples occupied this location as much as 6,000 years ago. Further evidence shows that in the year 985 or thereabouts an Icelandic trade ship bound for Greenland lost its way and went ashore here. Some 15 years later, Leif Eriksson wintered on a grassy terrace near present-day L'Anse aux Meadows.

It is believed that an Icelandic trade ship arrived on these shores in the year 985 when it was blown off course while on its way to Greenland. Norse contact continued until at least the mid-fourteenth century.

ABOVE: Native people began using this location some 6,000 years ago. Leif Eriksson wintered near here about 1,000 years ago. The present-day community of L'Anse aux Meadows was founded around 1835.

RIGHT: L'Anse aux Meadows' 1,000-year-old Viking colony is the first known European settlement in North America. Three timber-and-sod longhouses were constructed here, along with five smaller buildings. It may well be the first iron-working site on the North American continent.

LEFT: The Viking longhouse usually had one large room. Interior walls were lined with wood, or peat blocks in areas where there were few trees. The roof was covered with turf, which supplied remarkable protection from the elements.

In 1960 Norwegian archaeologists Helge Ingstad and Anne Stine Ingstad used Viking sagas in medieval Icelandic manuscripts and the help of local residents to locate the ruins of Straumfiord, Eriksson's settlement. Excavations revealed the remains of eight buildings and hundreds of Viking artifacts.

The site was designated a National Historic Site in 1978 and a UNESCO World Heritage Site in 1984.

19 MONTREAL JAZZ FESTIVAL
~ Quebec

The Montreal Jazz Festival (*Festival International de Jazz de Montréal*) is the largest jazz festival in the world, annually hosting around 500 concerts, some three-quarters of which are available free to the public.

Each summer, usually early in July, this culturally vibrant city blockades traffic in a section of its downtown core for almost two weeks as hundreds of musicians from all over the world perform on outdoor stages and in concert venues of all sizes for a combined audience of over two million people. Single outdoor concerts by artists such as Pat Metheny have been known to draw crowds of over 100,000.

The first Montreal Jazz Festival took place in 1980 and featured performances by Ray Charles, Vic Vogel, Chick Corea and Gary Burton. With an attendance of 12,000, the event was deemed a success. The annual two-week festival now attracts over two million people and is considered the largest jazz festival in the world.

Jazz legends Miles Davis, Dizzy Gillespie, Ella Fitzgerald, Stephane Grappelli, Chet Baker, Herbie Hancock, Antonio Carlos Jobim, Gil Evans, Dave Brubeck, Sonny Rollins, Chick Corea, Keith Jarrett, Oscar Peterson and many others have appeared regularly during the festival's history, but its remarkable success owes to its inclusion of younger jazz players such as Joshua Redmond, Roy Hargrove and Brad Mehldau; popular traditional jazz stars such as George Benson, Diana Krall and Michael Bublé; noted blues legends such as John Lee Hooker, Buddy Guy and B.B. King; mainstream pop acts such as Sting, Elvis Costello and Paul Simon; world musicians such as Milton Nascimento,

ABOVE: Larger festival concerts take place in major halls such as the Spectrum or those in Place des Arts, but many other performances take place in small- and medium-sized spaces with rich architectural history and marvelous acoustics. A personal favourite is the 425-seat amphitheatre of the Gesù Centre de Créativité, the oldest performance space in the city.

Burning Spear and Cesaria Evora; and Quebec's own prodigious talent, including Oliver Jones, Charlie Biddle and Guy Nadon. In other words: something for music lovers of all stripes.

Combine this unrivalled pool of eclectic musical talent with warm summer nights in the car-free heart of North America's most cosmopolitan city, and the livin' is easy. ∼

ABOVE: The festival is not only the largest of its kind, but arguably the most organized as well. Despite the fact that performances take place in dozens of venues, often with several happening simultaneously, the shows flow as smoothly as a well-oiled trombone. Lines are short and seemingly hundreds of bilingual volunteers are on hand to assist the lost or lingually confused.

20

MARY'S POINT
SHOREBIRD RESERVE
∼ New Brunswick

P art of the Shepody National Wilderness Area, Mary's Point Shorebird Reserve is one of the major migration stops for more than two million southbound shorebirds each year. In fact, the entire bay area has been declared a Western Hemispheric Shorebird Reserve.

The predominant species are semipalmated sandpipers, semipalmated plovers, ruddy turnstones, short-billed dowitchers, and greater and lesser yellowlegs. Somewhere between 75 to 95 percent of the world's population of semipalmated sandpipers depend on the Upper Bay of Fundy's mudflats for their survival during migration.

In order to fly the 4,000 kilometres (2,500 mi) non-stop to wintering grounds in South America, the birds must eat enough to double their body weight in two weeks.

BELOW The semipalmated (meaning partly web-footed) sandpiper constitutes as much as 95 percent of the migrating shorebird population that visits the Bay of Fundy region each summer.

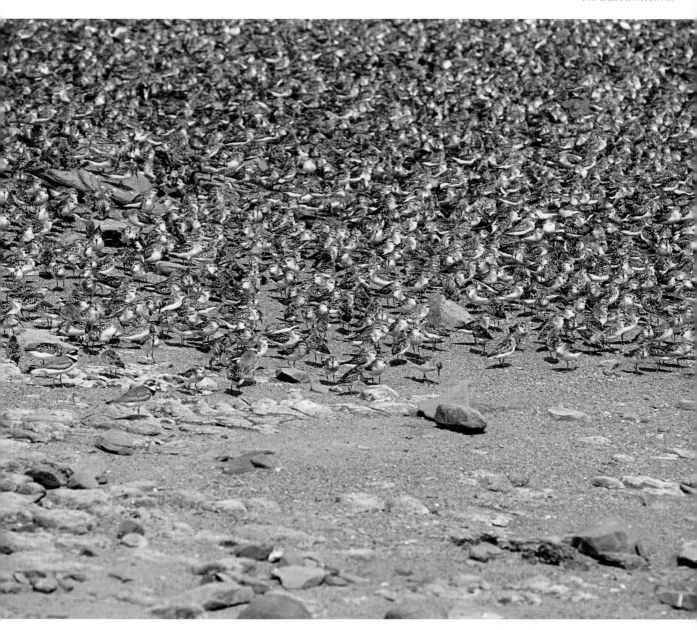

ABOVE: It's an amazing sight to see so many shorebirds in one location, but please keep in mind that any disturbance may cause them to move to a safer area, and each time they fly unnecessarily they burn up some of the fat reserves that they have stored for their migratory flight.

Semipalmated sandpipers and plovers spend early summer in Canada's sub-Arctic, but for six weeks or so every summer, Mary's Point becomes the shorebird capital of the Atlantic coast as the birds arrive to fatten themselves on the vast abundance of Fundy mud shrimp delivered twice daily by the receding tide. Each sandpiper can consume 10,000 to 20,000 of these tiny shrimp in a day. Only when they have doubled their weight will they have sufficient fat reserves to make the nonstop three-day flight to the northern coast of South America.

The best birdwatching time is from mid-July to mid-August. ⌒

21

MT. ROBSON PROVINCIAL PARK
∽ British Columbia

LEFT: Hikers following the Berg Lake Trail, which follows the Robson River from the south face to the north face, will discover more than 15 glaciers and numerous waterfalls before reaching Berg Lake at an elevation of 1628 metres (5,340 ft).

Towering above the Fraser Valley, at 3954 metres (12,972 ft) Mount Robson is the highest peak in the Canadian Rockies. Mount Robson Provincial Park is located in east-central British Columbia, just west of Alberta's Jasper National Park. The breathtaking scenery in the park makes it a perfect destination for hikers, climbers, and backcountry travellers. Wilderness, backcountry and walk-in camping are allowed in the park.

Mt. Robson was named in 1815 for Colin Robertson (mistranscribed as Robson), an employee of both the Hudson's Bay Company and the Northwest Company. The greater park area features 217,200 hectares (536,712 acres) of stunning mountains, valleys and waterways.

BELOW: Mt. Robson has been known at various times as Snow Cap Mountain and Cloud Cap Mountain, as its peak is often obscured by clouds even when fair weather prevails at lower levels. The region's Shuswap people are said to have referred to Mt. Robson as the "Mountain of the Spiral Road" due to the distinctive layers of rock that run around the mountain in a spiral pattern.

Birders have reported over 180 species in the park, and almost all wildlife species indigenous to the Rocky Mountains can be seen here. The park is one of the most undisturbed wilderness areas on the continent and offers excellent wildlife-viewing opportunities throughout. Mountain goats climb the many precarious cliffs and rockslides. Grizzlies and elk thrive at higher elevations, while elk and black bears inhabit the lower regions. Plentiful moose populations inhabit Moose Marsh. Nearby, Rearguard Falls on the Fraser River is the furthest migration point of the Pacific salmon.

Veteran surveyor Arthur Wheeler had this to say about his first sighting of Robson: "As we topped the crest the whole wonderful panorama came into view. At our feet flowed the Robson Glacier. Across the wide river of ice the great massif of Robson, rising supreme above all other peaks. White against a sky of perfect blue it seemed to belong to a world other than our own."

RIGHT: Prevailing westerly winds must rise to such heights to pass over the mountain that unusually heavy precipitation levels occur, and the result is a unique rainforest-like environment similar to that of the Coast Mountains.

The park is one of the most undisturbed wilderness areas on the continent.

BELOW: About an hour west of Jasper, Alberta, at the doorstep to Mt. Robson, Berg Lake is one of the most spectacular destinations in the Canadian Rockies. On a sunny day, its waters appear a vivid turquoise. Icebergs can be seen even in summer (hence the lake's name).

22 BIG MUDDY BADLANDS & the OUTLAW TRAIL
~ Saskatchewan

Butch Cassidy and the Sundance Kid, Dutch Henry and Sam Kelly's "Wild Bunch," a bad guy called "Bloody Knife," another called the "Pigeon Toe Kid," and Chief Sitting Bull...in Saskatchewan?!

The Big Muddy Badlands, a couple of hours south of Regina, about 19 kilometres (12 mi) south of Bengough on Highway 34, are the result of glacial action from the previous ice age. This rough landscape of gullies, caves and eroded sandstone outcrops stretches for 56 kilometres (35 mi) through border-country Saskatchewan into Montana. If you want to vanish into the landscape, this is the place to hide — or so the legends go.

After law came to the Wild West, the lawlessly inclined hightailed it north and holed up in the Big Muddy Badlands. Thieves, rustlers and smugglers from the United States disappeared across the border and used the Big Muddy's gullies and caves as bases from which to conduct their illegal activities.

ABOVE: The white-tailed deer is Saskatchewan's official animal. This native of the northern prairies is larger than its southern variant, weighing up to 180 kilograms (400 lbs).

LEFT: Characterized by deep gullies, weathered buttes and rough, desert-like scrubland covered in sage and cacti, the Big Muddy Badlands is a valley of eroded earth and sandstone along Big Muddy Creek. Native people who once lived here considered it a holy place.

ABOVE: Castle Butte, a 60-metre (196 ft) outcrop of compressed clay, rises suddenly from the surrounding landscape. Castle Butte's Ayer's-Rock-like presence on the relatively flat prairie announces the Big Muddy Badlands.

If you want to vanish
into the landscape,
this is the place to hide.

Bank robbers, bandits and others made use of the infamous Outlaw Trail, a network of sympathetic ranchers said to have been devised by Butch Cassidy and running all the way from Ciudad Juarez, Mexico, to the Big Muddy Badlands. Though there was a Mountie post nearby, the difficult terrain meant that the area was rarely patrolled.

The Sundance Kid is reported to have been a regular visitor to the area. Sitting Bull and his Sioux followers took refuge in the area after the Battle of Little Bighorn.

This is a visit with the Good, the Bad and the Muddy. Today's Highway 13, known as the Red Coat Trail, honours the North-West Mounted Police's role in the settlement of the Canadian West, while Highway 36 follows the original Outlaw Trail. Together with Highway 34, these roads encircle the historic Big Muddy Badlands. ⌁

23

ALGONQUIN PROVINCIAL PARK
~ Ontario

The rugged beauty of Algonquin Park became a national treasure in the early years of the twentieth century when members of the Group of Seven began travelling here to sketch and paint what they saw as a quintessentially Canadian landscape. Seeking to free themselves from the more conservative realistic style of landscape painting, the Group applied Impressionist techniques to evoke the vibrant colours of the near northern lakelands. In doing so, Algonquin Park became part of Canada's cultural history as well as its natural history.

LEFT: Algonquin is renowned for its maple hills, its rugged granite ridges, and its network of nearly countless waterways. A weekend spent paddling the outer lakes can be rejuvenating. A week or more spent exploring the interior lakes can be life-changing.

RIGHT: The moose is the unofficial symbol of Algonquin, though the park is home to 53 species of mammals, over 270 species of birds, and 30 species of reptiles and amphibians.

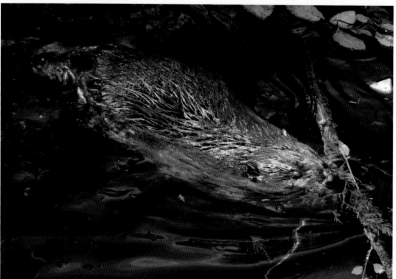

ABOVE: Because of its relative accessibility to southern Ontario's urban population, Algonquin Park can be a popular place in peak summer, so we recommend an autumn visit. That said, it's large enough that anyone willing to spend a day paddling and portaging into the interior lakes can experience a sense of wilderness.

LEFT: The beaver is vital to northern wilderness. By essentially building wetlands, it creates habitat for many different species. Beavers will attempt to construct dams any time they hear running water.

Situated in the transition zone between southern deciduous forests and northern coniferous forests, Algonquin Park vibrates with colour in autumn.

Tom Thomson will be forever associated with Algonquin, having served as a guide in the park and having done much of his painting on Canoe Lake, where he died under mysterious circumstances in 1917. A plaque honouring Thomson was erected at the Canoe Lake dock by the Historic Sites and Monuments Board of Canada.

The best way to explore Algonquin Park is by canoe. Paddle quietly down its rivers and along its lakeshores, and you are sure to see moose, deer, beaver and other of the more than 50 species of woodland mammals who call the park home. The park staff holds wolf-howling sessions in August. ～

The park features over 2000 kilometres (1,243 mi) of paddling possibilities, with routes suited to paddlers at all skill levels. There is no better way to explore Algonquin than by canoe.

24 WEST EDMONTON MALL
~ Alberta

Let's face it, some people would rather go to the mall than canoe the Nahanni or visit a Viking settlement. And in this case, going to the mall can be almost as breathtaking as many of Canada's natural wonders.

The West Edmonton Mall allows you to fulfill your consumer desires while visiting a wonder of the world (well, sort of). The Mall has been widely promoted as the "Eighth Wonder of the World" and is reported to be Alberta's biggest tourist draw.

The almost 50-hectare (123-acre) shopping centre houses over 800 stores and services and welcomes nearly 60,000 shoppers daily.

BELOW: Europa Boulevard is one of three grandly themed shopping areas, along with the New Orleans-like Bourbon Street area and a bustling indoor Chinatown. Europa Boulevard emulates the style of an Old World European city. Its boutiques offer fashions by leading designers and you can pause for cappuccino at the corner café.

ABOVE: At 2 hectares (5 acres) and with more than 20 aquatic activities, World Waterpark is said to be North America's largest indoor water park. It also has the world's largest wave pool. And even in the depths of an icy Edmonton winter, the temperature here remains a balmy 30 degrees Celsius (86°F) temperature.

ABOVE: Galaxyland's Mindbender is the world's largest indoor triple-loop rollercoaster, one of 25 rides and attractions in this part of the Mall. Construction is currently underway for a new rollercoaster designed for all ages. Galaxy Kids Playpark features four storeys of space-activities.

Beyond the mind-boggling shopping experience, you'll find the Mindbender, the world's largest indoor triple-loop roller-coaster, as well as North America's largest indoor water park, an indoor saltwater lake, a flock of flamingos, a casino, a full-scale concert venue, a dinner theatre, a shooting range, an indoor skateboarding park, an NHL-sized hockey rink, and a long list of other exciting attractions and distractions. The submarines are gone, replaced by a bumper-boat ride, but it's said that prior to 1998 the Mall owned more submarines than the Canadian Navy.

If it's still not big enough for you, stay tuned. The City of Edmonton recently granted the Mall permission to add even more retail space, a sports and convention facility, a 12-storey office tower, and a 600-unit apartment building.

25

CAPE BRETON HIGHLANDS & the CABOT TRAIL
⁓ Nova Scotia

LEFT: Cape Breton's northern highlands feature steep cliffs and densely forested plateaus overlooking the Atlantic.

Cape Breton Highlands National Park was established in 1936 as part of a system of national parks devised to protect outstanding Canadian landscapes. The park extends across the northern tip of Cape Breton Island, occupying almost 950 square kilometres (266 sq mi). It is the largest protected wilderness area in Nova Scotia, involving about 20 percent of the northern part of the island.

BELOW: The Cabot Trail is the best-known feature of Cape Breton Highlands National Park. It winds its way through the Gulf of St. Lawrence headlands and along the Atlantic shoreline, offering motorists and cyclists spectacular views around every turn.

The Micmac were the first people to fish along the gulf, preceding the Norse, the Portuguese, the French and the English. Cheticamp (above) comes from the Micmac word for "shallow harbour." The community has been strongly Acadian since the late 1700s.

Approximately a third of the famous highway known as the Cabot Trail winds through the park along the edge of 300-metre (985 ft) cliffs, in and out of dense hardwood and boreal forests, occasionally plunging deep into sheltered coves. It's a dream excursion for cyclists — *fit* cyclists.

Thirty additional natural-habitat trails branch off at various points along the national park section of the Cabot Trail.

The 298-kilometre (185-mi) Cabot Trail is named for merchant-explorer John Cabot, who is said to have landed on the Cape Breton coast and claimed it for England on June 24, 1497.

26

HISTORIC WHITEHORSE
~ Yukon

These are the basic facts: Whitehorse is Canada's largest community above 60 degrees north latitude. It is the capital city of the Yukon Territories. It is located on a river plain on the west side of the Yukon River about 100 kilometres (60 mi) north of the British Columbia–Yukon border. But we all know someone whose brother or sister or friend went to Whitehorse on a whim and stayed because they liked the "youthful, Wild West feel" of it. In some respects, Whitehorse is as much a feeling as it is a place.

Whitehorse lies mainly on the west side of the Yukon River. Many downtown businesses retain their Gold Rush-era appearance — brightly painted to attract new arrivals, fresh off the riverboat with money still in their pockets.

ABOVE: The sternwheeler S.S. *Klondike* was built in 1929. It sank in 1936 but was rebuilt and launched the following year as the *S.S. Klondike II*. The S.S. *Klondike* National Historic Site honours a vanished era of riverboat transportation on the Yukon River.

LEFT: The Frantic Follies revue celebrates the Great Klondike Gold Rush of 1898 with period music, can-can dancers, theatre and enthusiastic renditions of Robert Service's poetry.

Whitehorse was a key transportation hub and supply town during the famous Klondike Gold Rush. In 1900 the White Pass & Yukon Railway reached Whitehorse from Skagway, Alaska, and the town became a permanent settlement. Jack London was here. Robert Service began writing his rhyming verse here while working for the Bank of Commerce. Author Pierre Berton was born here. And though the Gold Rush days soon ended, giving way to a brief copper boom, a wartime airfield role, construction of the Alaska Highway, involvement in the Canol pipeline, and the perennial ups and downs of northern tourism, the city has maintained a prospector's optimism. Whitehorse remains a colourful destination, full of rowdy history and infectious charm.

The average age in Whitehorse is younger than that in most Canadian cities, and summer days can last almost 20 hours at this latitude. The residents of Whitehorse fill those days with a certain love of life — northern life — and they don't mind sharing. ᕐ

BELOW: Located at the head of navigation on the Yukon River, past two major obstacles, Miles Canyon and the Whitehorse Rapids, Whitehorse became a temporary stop-over for prospectors during the Klondike Gold Rush.

27

JUAN PEREZ SOUND & HOT SPRINGS ISLAND
～ British Columbia

LEFT: The diverse and abundant aquatic life in Perez Sound makes it a natural feeding ground for seals, sea lions, dolphins and whales.

Tucked into the eastern islands of Gwaii Haanas National Park Reserve and protected from the Pacific by Moresby Island's San Christoval Mountains, Juan Perez Sound offers an otherworldly calm. Its waters teem with marine life, from vibrantly coloured starfish, jellyfish and sea urchins to humpback, grey and killer whales, making it a kayaker's paradise.

The sound is named for Juan José Perez Hernández, who explored the Pacific coast on behalf of the viceroy of New Spain in 1774. It was Perez who named the San Cristobal (Christoval) Mountains.

BELOW: The 140-or-so islands of Gwaii Haanas are the stuff of kayakers' dreams. Visitors may find themselves awestruck by the region's combination of ancient forests, mountain vistas, secluded coves, countless species of birds and marine life, and wealth of Haida culture.

RIGHT: Migrating humpback and grey whales share Perez Sound waters with huge orcas and extremely active Pacific white-sided dolphins. The best time for whale-watching is in late spring and early summer.

BELOW: One-, two-, and three-week kayaking trips are available, as well as a nine-day schooner trip through the southern Haida Gwaii

RIGHT: Known to the Haida as Gandla K'in Gwaayaay, Hotspring Island is among the most popular destinations in the Queen Charlotte Islands. The island's hot springs are widely considered to be the most beautiful on the west coast.

The San Christoval Mountains (or San Cristobal) were named by Captain Juan Perez on his trip through the Queen Charlottes on behalf of New Spain in 1774.

Administration of Gwaii Haanas National Park is officially shared by Parks Canada and the Haida people. Hotspring Island in Perez Sound is one of five areas in the park supervised by members of the Haida nation. This island offers the perfect finish to a day spent kayaking the Sound. Just slip into one of three natural, earth-warmed, spring-fed rock pools and soak your tired body while soaking up the spectacular scenery.

This destination can be reached only by kayak, boat or float plane, but several reputable companies offer basic transportation or complete eco-tours. ✑

LEFT: Hotspring Island is renowned for its three descending volcanic pools: one atop a cliff, a second partway down, and a third at beach level. All offer the blissed-out bather a spectacular panoramic view of Perez Sound.

28

GATINEAU HOT-AIR BALLOON FESTIVAL
～ Quebec

LEFT: Hot-air balloons are pretty much at the mercy of prevailing winds, but wind direction and speed vary at different altitudes, so an experienced pilot can choose the right altitude to speed up, slow down or change course.

The Gatineau Hot-Air Balloon Festival was started by Jean Boileau in 1988. Today it is one of the biggest festivals in Canada, with an attendance of nearly 200,000 and over 100 balloons.

Each Labour Day weekend, spectators gather to gaze skyward as domestic participants and those from as many as 80 other nations employ a simple thermal principle to fill the horizon with colourful airborne shapes.

The French name for the festival is Le Festival de montgolfières de Gatineau. So balloons are *montgolfières*? Not exactly.

BELOW: Special shaped balloons are always a highlight of the festival. Some recent shapes have included an upside-down Humpty Dumpty (from Texas), a giant scarecrow (from Brazil), and a flying house (from Australia).

Meech Lake is located in
Gatineau Park, immediately
north of Gatineau at Chelsea
(the first municipality in Canada
to ban the use of pesticides).

Nearby Meech Lake is well known to most Canadians as a result of its 1987 role as the venue for talks over proposed changes to Canada's constitution (the Meech Lake Accord). A cottage is maintained here for the use of the Prime Minister of Canada.

Joseph and Étienne de Montgolfier were two of 16 children born to a paper manufacturer and his wife in a village south of Lyon, France. The brothers began their experiments with small hot-air balloons indoors in November 1782. On June 4, 1783, some 100 spectators watched as their 11-metre-wide (36 ft) silk-and-paper balloon rose into the sky and travelled 2 kilometres (1 1/4 mi) in 10 minutes before landing smoothly.

In September of that year, the Montgolfier brothers unveiled their latest creation for Louis XVI and a large crowd at Versailles. It was a large, elaborately painted, cotton-and-paper balloon with a rooster, a duck and a sheep aboard in a suspended cage. The balloon rose to an altitude of 500 metres (1,640 ft), travelled 3 kilometres (almost 2 mi) in 8 minutes, and returned the animals to earth unharmed. And that's how the Montgolfier name became part of the French language. ～

It isn't easy to inflate a hot-air balloon. It often takes a four-person team to accomplish the task. A crew competition is held each year to establish the fastest, most efficient ballooning team.

The annual festival also includes a major fireworks display and the Canadian finals for the Strongest Man Competition.

29

VIRGINIA FALLS
~ Northwest Territories

ABOVE: Perhaps a waterfall twice the height of Niagara Falls should be twice as hard to reach.

LEFT: In the centre of the Virginia Falls stands a spire of rock that has defied the erosion that has gradually moved the river upstream. It is known as Mason's Rock, after canoeist, artist, author and filmmaker Bill Mason

BELOW: The Slavey people and current Dene residents of Nahanni Butte know Virginia Falls simply as Nàilicho ("big falls").

Virginia Falls is almost twice as high as the far more famous Niagara Falls. This is where the wide, relatively tame South Nahanni River gets its reputation as wild water.

The river divides either side of a central pillar of rock known as Mason's Rock, for Canadian canoeing legend Bill Mason, before plunging roughly 90 metres (295 ft) to the canyon floor. Needless to say, it picks up a bit of speed.

Of course Virginia Falls could be Trudeau Falls by the time you read this. Proposals have been made. Our former prime minister loved the Nahanni. He advocated for its designation as a national park. And on some level it makes sense to put his name to it. But here's the story behind Virginia Falls' name:

Virginia Hunter's father, a New York businessman who made his money from trolley-car signs, came back from one of his many northern trips to announce that he was leaving her mother. The story goes that teenaged Virginia saw her father only once more after that devastating visit. Fenley Hunter was not a father to be proud of, but he did leave a lasting impression by naming one of Canada's most remarkable geographical features for his daughter. In his diary he wrote, "I wish Virginia could see them, as I have named them after her." His rudimentary survey proved that he knew the exact location of the falls, and in 1930 the Geographic Board of Canada approved the name. Virginia passed away in 1997 in a retirement village in Pennsylvania. She never saw her namesake falls. They were as distant as her father. ~

FOLLOWING PAGES: Colourful Painted Canyon stretches downstream from below Virginia Falls, allowing the reunited waters of the South Nahanni speedy passage. A portage trail of moderate difficulty leads to the base of the falls.

30 PRINCE EDWARD ISLAND NATIONAL PARK
∾ Prince Edward Island

One of Canada's smallest national parks, Prince Edward Island National Park extends 40 kilometres (25 mi) from Cavendish to Dalvay along the island's north shore and about 6 kilometres (4 mi) along the western tip of Greenwich Peninsula. The park's striking red sandstone cliffs, remarkable network of dunes and beaches, and Gulf Stream-warmed waters beckon visitors from all over the world.

RIGHT: Dunes are created when sand is deposited behind rocks, seaweed or other plant life on the beach. They then continue to build slowly with the effects of wind and waves. Tenacious, rough-bladed marram grass thrives on the Island's shores and acts as a net in catching and accumulating sand deposits.

BELOW: PEI's rugged coastline features long stretches of red sandstone cliffs. Though the rock was formed 285 million years ago, it is constantly being reshaped by erosion.

ABOVE: The dunes are home to many animals, including the sprightly red fox, which probably benefits from the camouflaging colours of the surrounding sandstone.

RIGHT: Cavendish Beach is one of PEI's widest and most popular, but even in peak tourist season, it's relatively easy to find a dune of one's own.

The land within the park's boundaries
was once home to Mi'kmaq people,
Acadian fishermen and British farmers.
It became a holiday destination
in the late 1800s.

The area was designated a national park in 1937, but the western tip of Greenwich Peninsula was added in 1998 in an attempt to protect and preserve the area's fragile coastal dune system as well as its historical importance. (Stone tools and other objects uncovered at adjacent St. Peter's Bay date back over 10,000 years.) The Greenwich Dunes Trail highlights the crescent-shaped dunes and their migrating ridges.

In this section of the park, visitors should follow designated paths and take note of wildlife protection zones. ∾

RIGHT: PEI National Park boasts over 300 species of birds, including the great blue heron and the endangered piping plover.

31

HEAD-SMASHED-IN BUFFALO JUMP
~ Alberta

For almost 6,000 years, hunters surrounded the buffalo herds at their grazing grounds in the Porcupine Hills, west of the cliffs at Head-Smashed-In Buffalo Jump, gathered the bison into lanes lined with hundreds of stone cairns, and drove them at full speed toward the "jump." The buffalo jump was a cliff about 300 metres (328 yd) long and over 10 metres (33 ft) high. The buffalo simply could not stop in time to save themselves. The carcasses were dealt with at a nearby camp: skinned for the hides that would be used to create clothing and shelter; butchered for meat; and bones and horns set aside for tool-making.

The site was first excavated by the American Museum of Natural History in 1938. Archaeologists estimate that the area's aboriginal people used this site as a buffalo jump for almost 6,000 years. Skeletal remains were discovered to be 10 metres (33 ft) deep in places.

While the use of buffalo jumps was common among early plains people, Head-Smashed-In is considered to be among the world's oldest, largest and best-preserved jump sites. As such, it was designated a Canadian National Historic Site in 1968, a Provincial Historic Site in 1979, and a UNESCO World Heritage Site in 1981. ~

ABOVE: Head-Smashed-In boasts a $10-million interpretive centre built into a sandstone cliff. Exhibits on five levels depict various aspects of early Blackfoot life on the high plains, the buffalo hunt, and the archaeological methods used to unearth artifacts and explain a vanished way of life.

LEFT: Located about 18 kilometres (11 mi) northwest of Fort MacLeod, Alberta, Head-Smashed-In Buffalo Jump is perhaps the oldest and best-preserved example of a bison-hunting jump in the world.

RIGHT: Combining their knowledge of local terrain and bison behaviour, generations of aboriginal hunters were able to stampede their quarry over these cliffs and thereby feed and clothe themselves and their families for almost 6,000 years.

32

CN TOWER
⁓ Ontario

LEFT: Over 1,500 workers were employed in construction of Toronto's CN Tower. Its main structure is composed of almost 130 kilometres (80 mi) of tensioned steel and 40,525 cubic metres (53,005 cu yd) of concrete. It is widely considered to be the most elegant of the world's large communications towers.

While Canada's largest city has no shortage of unique architecture, both heritage and modern, its most recognizable structure is the CN Tower. Defining the Toronto skyline at a height of 553.33 metres (1,815.5 ft), the CN Tower is widely embraced as Canada's national tower, the world's tallest free-standing tower for over 32 years. This engineering wonder dominates the city's harbourfront skyline and draws almost two million visitors a year from around the globe.

The Tower was built between 1973 and 1976 for the Canadian National Railway and cost upward of $63 million at the time. In 1995 the Tower was declared one of the Seven Wonders of the Modern World by the American Society of Civil Engineers, joining such notable landmarks as the Channel Tunnel, the Panama Canal and the Golden Gate Bridge.

BELOW: The CN Tower's four observation levels offer amazing views of Toronto, day and night. The Glass Floor and Outdoor Observation Deck is found at 342 metres (1,122 ft). Next is the Look-Out Level at 346 metres (1,136 ft). The tower's famous revolving restaurant, 360, overlooks the city from a height of 351 metres (1,151 ft) and offers diners both award-winning cuisine and constantly changing views. And the Sky Pod, the Tower's public observation deck, looks down on Ontario's capital city from a height of 447 metres (1,465 ft).

ABOVE: At 553 metres (1,815.5 ft), the Tower is almost twice as tall as the Eiffel Tower.

LEFT: During peak season some 550 people staff the Tower, its restaurants and its entertainment facilities.

Travelling at approximately 6 metres (20 ft) per second, the Tower's glass-fronted elevators whisk guests to the top in just 58 seconds.

The Tower was proposed as a solution to television reception problems in 1960s Toronto. As the number of skyscrapers in the city grew, radio and television signals were increasingly deflected during transmission. In a bold effort to solve the problem and make headlines, CN decided to raise the tallest telecommunications tower in history.

Concrete for the foundation was poured 24 hours a day for almost four months. As each section hardened, the molds were raised and tapered. The base of the Tower is formed by hollow Y-shaped legs. Though each leg is hollow, the concrete that surrounds it is some 7 metres (23 ft) thick.

Today, the Tower's microwave telecommunications receptors at 338 metres (1,109 ft) allow Torontonians to enjoy remarkably clear reception, among the best in North America. ～

33 CIRQUE of the UNCLIMBABLES
~ Northwest Territories

The Cirque of the Unclimbables is a daunting collection of 610-metre (2,000 ft) vertical cliffs accessible only by water or air (usually by floatplane). The flight in offers striking views of Mt. Harrison Smith, Mt. Proboscis and the Lotus Flower Tower. With its 762-metre (2,500 ft) continuous crack system and 22 pitches, Lotus Flower Tower is one of the most famous of the "Fifty Classic Climbs of North America."

The name Cirque of the Unclimbables is said to have been coined by mountaineer Arnold Wexler in 1955. His 1956 article in the *American Alpine Journal* caused climbers from all over the globe to set their sights on this remote, undeveloped cluster of peaks.

Geologically speaking, a *cirque* is a steep-walled, semi-circular basin formed by glacial erosion at the head of a mountain valley. *Unclimbable* means…well, nothing entices climbers like the word *unclimbable*. ~

RIGHT and FOLLOWING PAGES: The glaciers seen from the air on the way into the Cirque are over a million years old. Temperatures here can drop to -70 degrees Celsius (-94° F).

BELOW: The Cirque of the Unclimbables is located upstream from Nahanni National Park Reserve, a World Heritage Site. A century ago, prospectors came to this region in search of gold. They found very little of it, but they did experience some of the most varied and awe-inspiring scenery in the world — towering peaks and tundra, sand dunes and wetland bogs.

34

GRASSLANDS NATIONAL PARK
~ Saskatchewan

Grasslands National Park comprises two relatively pristine areas of mixed-grass prairie along the Montana–Saskatchewan border. The park is one of 39 regions across the country to be preserved as a Natural Region of Canada. This Prairie Grasslands Natural Region features indigenous varieties of long and short grasses inhabited by indigenous prairie wildlife.

The eastern branch of the park features the Killdeer badlands, where exposed rock shows 60,000 years of geological history. The western branch features the dramatic Frenchman River Valley and its highlight, 70 Mile Butte. This isn't checkerboard-farmland Saskatchewan. The view from 70 Mile Butte reveals a vast, rugged landscape of coulees, creeks and buttes straight out of a Wild West movie.

As much as 18,000 years ago, ancestors of the Assiniboine, Cree and Blackfoot hunted buffalo here. Native artifacts have been discovered at approximately 3,000 sites.

Though archaeologists have discovered evidence of Native life dating back thousands of years in the region, it has taken only a century of settlement to make the natural prairie grasslands an endangered habitat and to threaten the survival of much of its wildlife. Under the current plan, Grasslands National Park will expand as additional ranchlands become available for purchase. ∼

LEFT: Grasslands National Park and the region immediately surrounding it are the only places in Canada to see colonies of black-tailed prairie dogs.

ABOVE: Human settlement and the resulting disruption of habitat caused the near extinction of several prairie species in the previous century. The pronghorn antelope was among them, but conservation efforts have made the pronghorn a common sight again in Grasslands National Park.

LEFT: A once common prairie-dweller now on the province's endangered species list, the burrowing owl nests in underground dens previously inhabited by gophers, prairie dogs and badgers.

35

WITLESS BAY ECOLOGICAL RESERVE
~ Newfoundland and Labrador

LEFT: In order to protect the seabirds' nesting grounds, visitors should approach the reserve's islands aboard licensed tour boats. Landing on the islands is prohibited without a scientific research or special access permit.

Just off the east coast of Newfoundland's Avalon Peninsula are the four birds-only islands of the Witless Bay Ecological Reserve. Gull, Green, Great and Pee Pee Island are the summer home of North America's largest Atlantic puffin colony. About 95 percent of North America's puffin population returns each year to breed off the coasts of Newfoundland and Labrador, and this is their favourite spot. It's estimated that more than 260,000 pairs nest here during the late spring and summer.

BELOW: Puffins feed by diving for small fish, usually catching up to 10 at a time. They have been known to dive to depths of 60 metres (200 ft) and remain underwater for up to a minute.

RIGHT: The Witless Bay islands are part of the Maritime Barrens—Southeastern Barrens sub-region. They were designated a wildlife reserve in 1964 and an ecological reserve in 1983.

BELOW: Many reputable tour-boat companies operate out of coastal villages near the islands. These boats also cruise for icebergs and whales in season.

ABOVE: The many coves, sea caves and arches found offshore delight kayakers. Kayak rentals and tours are available from most area harbours.

You will also see thousands of small, black birds with white rumps. These are Leach's storm-petrels, named for British zoologist William Leach. The islands host the world's second-largest Leach's storm-petrel colony, more than 620,000 pairs. The small, plump-looking gulls perched by the thousands on every available cliff edge are black-legged kittiwakes. And the birds that when standing erect resemble miniature penguins are common murres, known outside North America as common guillemots.

This is a great trip just for the birdwatching, but if your timing is right, you can also see icebergs and whales. ⌒

LEFT: Atlantic puffins are monogamous and both parents provide care for the young. Their bright orange bills are actually attractive plates employed during mating season. After mating, these bill plates are shed as the mated pair bang their beaks together.

36

THE INSIDE PASSAGE
~ British Columbia

The Inside Passage is the passage less travelled. It wasn't until 1996 that B.C. Ferries initiated its Discovery Coast Passage service between Vancouver Island's Port Hardy and the province's northernmost port of Prince Rupert. This route makes use of the relatively sheltered waters of the central and northern coastlines, and offers passengers hours of spectacular coastal scenery.

ABOVE: Watch for whales and dolphins in Queen Charlotte Sound during the summer months, and for cream-coloured "spirit bears" along Princess Royal Island's shoreline. These are Kermode bears, a distinct subspecies of black bear possessing a recessive trait that causes a small percentage to be born with light-coloured coats.

LEFT: Until B.C. Ferries launched the Discovery Coast Passage run in 1996, the province's central coast was largely inaccessible by water.

ABOVE: The Discovery Coast Passage travels through B.C.'s central coast archipelago via a narrow maze of channels, passes and reaches. For much of the trip, the coastal mountains plunge directly into the Pacific.

For centuries, Native people enjoyed the region's abundant sources of food and its moderate climate, which allowed them to create permanent, culturally rich settlements, in contrast to the nomadic lifestyles of most other hunter-gather societies. What limited travel they did was accomplished in large dugout canoes through these same waters.

Today, several cruise lines use the 507-kilometre (314 mi) Inside Passage en route to Alaska, and B.C. Ferries operates a year-round service between Port Hardy and Prince Rupert. The trip is very popular during the summer months, and if you intend to take your vehicle, reservations are strongly advised. 〜

LEFT: *The Queen of Prince Rupert* operates on the Inside Passage during low season and passes her duties to the M.V. *Northern Adventure* during the high season.

37

POINTE-AU-PÈRE LIGHTHOUSE
⁓ Quebec

Pointe-au-Père's maritime history extends back some 200 years, and the best way to learn about its role in many key events on the St. Lawrence is to visit its 1909 lighthouse, now part of the Musée de la Mer (Museum of the Sea). This third-of-four lighthouses is part of the Pointe-au-Père National Historic Site.

Though no longer active, the lighthouse stands the second-tallest in Canada. The world's first fog-alarm systems were tested here, and in a time before airmail, transatlantic vessels dropped mailbags at this lighthouse for distribution to destinations across the continent via boat, train or truck.

Pointe-au-Père's Marconi telegraph station was used to alert police that Dr. Hawley Harvey Crippen, fleeing Britain for the United States after murdering his wife, was aboard a ship entering Canadian (British Crown dominion) waters. Crippen shortly thereafter became the first criminal to be captured with the aid of wireless communication.

At 33 metres (108 ft), Pointe-au-Père Lighthouse is the second-tallest in Canada, a 128-step climb to the top. Built in 1909, it was replaced by an electronic lighthouse in 1975.

ABOVE: The light was not enough in May 1914 when the Canadian Pacific passenger liner *Empress of Ireland* collided with a Norwegian coal freighter in thick fog and sank in just 14 minutes. Some 1,012 passengers and crew perished in the disaster, more than in the sinking of the *Titanic*.

The lighthouse both prevented and witnessed numerous shipwrecks in its day. Among the latter was the sinking of the *Empress of Ireland* in 1914, when more lives were lost than in the sinking of the *Titanic*. Musée de la Mer exhibits recount this and other tales of early St. Lawrence River history. ⟿

LEFT: The lighthouse was built to guide ships safely along the often foggy shores of the St. Lawrence River. The waters became safer still in 1909 when Pointe-au-Père became home to the new Marconi wire telegraph station.

38

AGAWA CANYON
~ Ontario

LEFT: At 68.5 metres (225 ft), Bridal Veil Falls is the highest in Agawa Canyon Wilderness Park. Five nature trails crisscross the park, and a lookout located 370 steps up the wall of the canyon provides a panoramic view.

BELOW: The Algoma Central Railway provides a drop-off service for canoeists and kayakers. An Agawa Canyon Tour Train takes hikers to the canyon floor for two hours of exploration before returning to the station.

Agawa Canyon Wilderness Park is located approximately 183 kilometres (114 mi) northwest of Sault Ste. Marie in Ontario's Algoma District and is accessible only by hiking trail or the historic Algoma Central Railway.

The bedrock beneath the canyon is part of the Canadian Shield, formed some 2.5 billion years ago. It is among the oldest rock on Earth. The canyon was created more than a billion years ago, the result of faulting along the Shield. The canyon's walls reach 175 metres (575 ft) at their highest point, and four waterfalls spill into the Agawa River from the canyon's rim: Otter Creek Falls, North and South Black Beaver Falls, and the highest, Bridal Veil Falls.

Several members of the Group of Seven — Lawren Harris, A.Y. Jackson, Frank Johnston, A.E.H. MacDonald and Arthur Lismer — were captivated by Agawa's rugged beauty and painted here between 1918 and 1923. They travelled to their favourite Agawa locations aboard a specially outfitted Algoma Central boxcar.

Various train tours are offered throughout the year, including a popular Fall Colours Tour and a winter Snow Train Tour. ~

39

NAHANNI NATIONAL PARK RESERVE
~ Northwest Territories

For many Canadians of a certain age, the Nahanni region came into the public eye in the early 1970s when Prime Minister Pierre Trudeau canoed the river and met with Native leaders regarding Nahanni's potential designation as a national park. In 1972 the Government of Canada established the Nahanni National Park Reserve, and in 1978 the park became the first UNESCO World Heritage Site to receive its status based on its importance as a natural heritage site. Since that time the name Nahanni has been almost synonymous with "wild."

LEFT: The South Nahanni River begins as a simple stream in the Mackenzie Mountains, but as it makes its way 580 kilometres (360 mi) downstream through a series of deep canyons it widens, picks up speed, and earns its reputation as one of the world's premier wilderness rivers.

RIGHT: The South Nahanni River is a top canoeing destination, but due to its remoteness it sees fewer than 800 paddlers a year. With challenging whitewater, towering canyons and spectacular waterfalls, the South Nahanni was designated a Canadian Heritage River in 1987.

RIGHT: Both black bears and grizzlies reside in Nahanni Reserve. Bear attacks are uncommon, as wild animals generally prefer to avoid contact with humans, but it never hurts to brush up on your bear-encounter etiquette.

BELOW: Make no mistake, Nahanni is a whitewater river with whirlpools, eddies, boils, riffles and figure-eight rapids at a place called "Hell's Gate." The occasional portage might be prudent.

This is a wilderness largely unaltered by humans, and because Nahanni escaped the smoothing effects of glaciation during the last ice age, its canyon walls are steep and rugged.

There are no roads or settlements. This is the wilderness. Nahanni National Park Reserve is a near-pristine example of north country's rivers, canyons, forests and tundra.

Among the park's many outstanding features are Virginia Falls (twice as high as Niagara Falls), the four canyons below it (with vertical walls reaching 1,200 metres [3,937 ft]), Rabbitkettle Hotsprings (source of the largest tufa mounds in Canada), and the unusual karst formations of the Ram Plateau.

For diehard adventurers, there are a number of ambitious overland routes into the park, but the vast majority of visitors arrive via floatplane at either Virginia Falls or Rabbitkettle Lake, the only designated aircraft landing sites. Canoeists can begin outside the park at the river's headwaters, a location known as the Moose Ponds. A day's paddling takes you from stream to wide river to "the Rock Garden," a tamely named section of wild whitewater featuring Class II and III rapids.

Where the water slows, watch for wolves, bears, woodland caribou, Dall's sheep and mountain goats. Nahanni National Park Reserve is home to a variety of northern wildlife. ～

40

BAFFIN ISLAND
～ Nunavut

Baffin Island is the largest island in Canada and the fifth-largest island in the world — more than four and a half times the size of Newfoundland. In fact, three of the world's ten largest islands are found in Canada's Arctic Archipelago.

Though Canada is a northern country, few Canadians ever make it to *the* North — a rugged, tale-worthy land that indigenous peoples have inhabited for millennia. Evidence of Pre-Dorset culture dating back 4,000 years was found on the north end of the Baffin Island. These Paleoeskimos were succeeded by the Dorset culture, and the Dorset by the Thule, ancestors of modern Inuit.

Baffin Island is believed to have been visited by Vikings in the eleventh century. The island's size and its almost countless fjords confused several early explorers who came in search of the Northwest Passage. British explorer Martin Frobisher visited the island three times between 1576 and 1578.

ABOVE: Qikiqtarjuaq (formerly Broughton Island) offers excellent chances of viewing narwhal, beluga, right and killer whales, and walrus.

BELOW: It is widely believed that Baffin Island was visited by Norse explorers early in the eleventh century. Some scholars believe that the island is the "Helluland" referred to in the Viking sagas.

ABOVE: Looking along the Cumberland Peninsula shore-line toward Cape Dyer. The invisible Arctic Circle cuts across Cape Dyer on its way to (or from) Greenland.

BELOW: *Inukshuk* means "in the image of a person" in the Inuktitut language. Traditionally, the Inuit created these stone figures to provide directions for travellers or hunters, warn them of danger, or mark sacred sites. Inuit tradition forbids the destruction of an inukshuk.

Frobisher Bay separates Hall Peninsula from Meta Incognita Peninsula on the southeast end of the island. The territorial capital, Iqaluit, is located where these two peninsulas meet. The island itself is named for another British explorer, William Baffin, who in 1616, along with Robert Bylot, mapped Baffin Island and discovered Lancaster Sound off Baffin's northwestern tip.

The western side of the island is largely tundra. The east features snow-capped mountains, some of which stand more than 2,440 metres (8,000 ft). Most of the island's inhabitants are Inuit and live near the coastal trading posts. All communities north of tourist-friendly Pangnirtung experience the Midnight Sun (round-the-clock daylight from mid-May to the end of June) and Polar Night (when the sun sets in late November and does not rise again until mid-January). ⁓

41

PACIFIC RIM
NATIONAL PARK RESERVE
~ British Columbia

LEFT: The wild forces of Nature so visibly displayed along the Pacific Rim shoreline can be somehow simultaneously ferocious and calming.

Pacific Rim National Park is the only national park on Vancouver Island. This magnificent collection of trails, beaches, islands and ocean was set aside in 1970 in an effort to preserve unique rainforest and marine habitat.

For thousands of years, the Nuu-chah-nulth people were the only residents of this remote coastal landscape and its verdant forests. Today, roughly a million people arrive each year to shed the tensions of urban life and recharge their spiritual batteries. But don't expect to be part of a crowd when you visit. The park is so large and its forests so dense that you can go for hours without encountering a fellow adventurer.

The park encompasses almost 50,000 hectares (123,550 acres) divided into three geographic locations: Long Beach, the Broken Group Islands and the West Coast Trail.

Long Beach is perhaps the most popular and most easily accessible of the three. The expansive beaches of Schooner Cove, Wickaninnish and Florencia Bays, collectively known as Long Beach, connect the villages of Tofino and Ucluelet. Radar Hill, just south of Tofino, offers a spectacular view of Tofino Inlet, Meares Island and Gowlland Rocks.

BELOW: The annual rainfall in the park is 270 centimetres (106 in). July and August offer the most sunshine, but waterproof clothing and camping gear are a must.

ABOVE: The rainforest climate in Pacific Rim Park is perfect for cedar, hemlock, fir and spruce. Beneath the canopy, the forest floor runs thick with berry bushes, mosses, lichens and fungi.

Long Beach caters to visitors seeking to relax in the picnic areas, comb the beaches or stroll along the trails and boardwalks.

LEFT: Ocher starfish are the most abundant type found in the intertidal zone. They are generally a shade of purple, brown or yellow.

ABOVE: It is possible to view sea lions, Pacific gray whales and killer whales just offshore from the trail. Black bears routinely inspect the tidal flats for the lush variety of seafood delivered twice daily.

The Broken Group Islands are a collection of over 100 islands, islets and outcrops located in Barkley Sound. This is a perfect place to kayak, camp and generally escape into some of the most beautiful and secluded scenery on the planet.

Pacific Rim's West Coast Trail has been called "the best hike in the world." If not the best, it must certainly rank near the top of any objective list. This challenging 77-kilometre (47 mi) trail connects the communities of Port Renfrew and Bamfield on Vancouver Island's southwest coast. En route are lush rainforests, spectacular headland lookouts, pristine beaches, hidden lagoons and no shortage of wildlife viewing opportunities. The West Coast Trail is by no means an easy stroll along the beach, but it rewards tenacious trekkers with its seemingly endless variations of green quietude and breathtaking ocean vistas. The trail is open from May 1 to September 30. ⌒

LEFT: Much of the West Coast Trail traces a century-old rescue route developed following the tragic wreck of the S.S. *Valencia*, which ran aground in a severe storm in 1906, losing all passengers and crew. This section of the Pacific saw more than 60 shipwrecks between 1854 and 1906.

42

PEGGY'S COVE
~ Nova Scotia

The small post office in the lighthouse's lower level serves as the village post office during summer months.

The village of Peggy's Cove possesses that indefinable Atlantic charm. It remains a working fishing village, but in summer, its docks and rocks brim with tourists. In attempt to preserve its rugged beauty, an act was passed in 1962 to govern any new development in and around the village, including neighbouring barrens, bogs, ponds and coastline.

Part of the Lighthouse Trail Drive, Peggy's Cove lighthouse is said to be one of the most photographed structures in Atlantic Canada. The first lighthouse was built here in 1868 to mark the eastern entrance to St. Margaret's Bay. This beacon-atop-a-house was replaced by the current 15-metre (50 ft), octagonal, iron-and-concrete lighthouse in 1914. The lighthouse was used by the Navy as a radio communications centre during the Second World War.

Ocean currents from both Arctic and tropical waters bring an unusual combination of sea creatures near the shores of Peggy's Cove, including dolphins, seals and bluefin tuna, as well as rare and endangered species such as right whales and Atlantic leatherback sea turtles. ~

ABOVE: At the end of the last ice age, as the ice sheet retreated, boulders known as glacial erratics were carried and deposited across the maritime landscape. These large "erratic" boulders create a fascinating shoreline of stone.

RIGHT: In 1811 the Province of Nova Scotia granted six families the over 800 acres of land that would become the village of Peggy's Cove. The community soon grew in population and businesses. These included a general store, several fish-processing houses and a lobster-processing facility.

LEFT: The previous wooden lighthouse served as keeper's quarters until it was badly damaged by Hurricane Edna in 1954. Since its automation in 1958, the original red light has been changed to a white beacon and, since the late 1970s, to green.

43 The RAM PLATEAU
~ Northwest Territories

The Ram Plateau is part of the Mackenzie Mountains, west of Fort Simpson and north of Nahanni National Park Reserve. Many of the plateau's towers resemble high plains mesas, the backdrop for a film set in the Wild West. On closer inspection, the Ram's towers and canyon walls are higher and steeper than they originally appear: reaching 1800 metres (5,900 ft) in places, plunging at startling angles to the Ram River below.

The Ram Plateau is located outside Nahanni National Park Reserve, but there have been strong recommendations for the inclusion of Ram and its karstlands in an expanded park.

ABOVE: Some canyon walls in the Ram Plateau region dive 1800 metres (5,900 ft), and much of the area's rock displays remarkable karst formations — caves, sinkholes and passages created as water methodically erodes limestone over time.

Visitors are encouraged to practise leave-no-trace trekking and camping in this untarnished ecosystem.

Over millennia, water has had its way with this limestone landscape. The land rose and water rushed, flowed and trickled downward, creating cliffs, hoodoos, caves of all shapes and sizes, elaborate tunnels, visible channels, underground passageways, basins, sinkholes and eerie, otherworldly karst formations.

The Ram Plateau offers hikers a chance to explore thousands of years of geology in a single destination — a lost world near one of Canada's most famous national parks. ⤳

LEFT: Caribou, mountain goats and Dall's sheep are frequently sighted.

44 CANADA DAY in OTTAWA
～ Ontario

Summer is in full stride, it's the nation's birthday, and there really is no better place to be than Ottawa.

Despite Canada's geographical status as the second-largest country on Earth, Canada Day celebrations in Ottawa offer a comforting reminder that we have more in common with Switzerland or Sweden than with our powerful neighbour to the south. Our modest population has chosen, as a society, to embrace a polite, peaceful orderliness that makes it possible on July 1 to meet and speak to the Governor-General, to stand just an arm's length from the Prime Minister, and to rub shoulders with the country's most famous scientists, athletes, literary figures, musicians, actors and television personalities as we all celebrate together.

Aside from expressing enthusiasm at international hockey contests, there aren't many occasions when Canadians feel right about public displays of patriotic pride — Canada Day in Ottawa is the right time and place.

Crowds of over 300,000 gather at key locations such as Major's Hill Park and Jacques-Cartier Park to watch the year's grandest fireworks exhibition. Much of the downtown area, as well as the du Portage bridge and all of Laurier Street in Hull, is closed to traffic as the capital city looks to the night sky.

ABOVE: Parliament Hill is the focal point for the day's activities. Performers from every province and territory take turns entertaining the thousands of Canadians who gather together family-picnic-style on the vast lawn.

If you can't be here, the day's main events are broadcast and webcast live throughout the country and abroad. But no matter where in Canada you call home, you should try to attend at least one Canada Day celebration in the nation's capital. The collective spirit is electric, and the patriotic wave that swells through the crowds is decidedly more thankful than boastful. This is a great country.

Watch the parade along Elgin Street from a prime spot in Gatineau Park. Take part in the multi-cultural activities at the World Pavilion in Rideau Falls Park. Tour the Governor-General's residence, Rideau Hall. See the changing of the guard. Watch the RCMP musical ride. Look up to catch the Snowbirds flying in formation. Visit museums and other attractions for free. Enjoy the countless buskers and street performers, in addition to the dozens of acts on the Parliament Hill main stage. And, around 10:00 PM, be sure to find a comfortable spot to witness the spectacular fireworks as they rise above the Ottawa River, fill the sky and frame the Peace Tower.

LEFT: No matter where you look, the city is red and white. The red maple leaf is proudly displayed on flags of all sizes, banners and pennants, t-shirts and bathing suits, balloons and pinwheels, beanies and ball caps, and tattoos (both temporary and permanent).

45

GULF ISLANDS
NATIONAL PARK RESERVE
~ British Columbia

When people refer to the Gulf Islands, they generally mean the larger Gulf Islands in the southern half of the Strait of Georgia — Saltspring, Mayne, North and South Pender, Galiano, Saturna. Denman, Hornby, Gabriola, Valdes….

In 2003 Gulf Islands National Park Reserve became Canada's first new national park reserve of the twenty-first century when it was established to protect the region's ecological integrity in the face of rapid population growth and residential and resort development. The park is spread over representative sections of 15 islands, as well as several islets, reefs and marine areas.

ABOVE: The Mediterranean-like climate of the southern Gulf Islands permits the survival of plants found nowhere else in Canada. The arbutus, with its shedding bark and distinctly smooth skin beneath, is the only native broadleaf evergreen tree in Canada.

The Gulf Islands are located in a seismically active area. This doesn't mean regularly erupting volcanoes, just that the routine movement of local tectonic plates accounts for the islands' beautiful high ridges and deep, narrow valleys.

Contrary to the popularly held notion that the region is one big rainforest, the southern islands experience warm, dry summers. Salish-speaking people used these islands for thousands of years, moving with the seasons, harvesting the sea and intertidal zones, gathering plants for a wide range of uses. It wasn't until the late 1800s that European settlers arrived and commenced clearing land for towns and farms.

LEFT: B.C. Ferries operates regular ferry service between the Lower Mainland, Vancouver Island and the Gulf Islands. In addition, a number of tour companies offer day trips and overnight excursion tours to these laidback, picturesque islands.

ABOVE: Though still tourist-friendly, the islands have become a popular retirement location. Saltspring Island real estate is among the most expensive in Canada.

Fishing, logging and small-scale agriculture remain economically important to the Gulf Islands, but in recent years recreation and tourism have assumed an increasingly greater role. The islands perhaps boast more artists and artisans per capita than any other region of Canada. Natural and crafted beauty seem to go hand in hand in the Gulf Islands. ⌇

RIGHT: The Salish lived in these islands for thousands of years before Spanish explorers began mapping them in the 1700s. European settlers didn't arrive in significant numbers until the late 1800s. Today, the southern Gulf Islands are among the most prized residential and resort locations in Canada.

46

BAY of FUNDY TIDES
~ New Brunswick

Bay of Fundy tides rise five times higher than the average for all Atlantic tides.

During one tide cycle, an estimated 100 billion tons of seawater flows in and out of the Bay of Fundy. That's more than the combined flow of all the world's freshwater rivers.

New Brunswick isn't the only place to experience Fundy's record-topping tides (many harbours in Nova Scotia share this feat of nature), but the shores of Fundy National Park and neighbouring mudflats at Hopewell Rocks offer perhaps the most spectacular experience.

The upper basins of the Bay of Fundy have a tidal fluctuation of around 15 metres (50 ft), or five times higher than typical Atlantic coast tides. Each 24-hours brings two high and two low tides. The time between a high tide and a low tide averages about 6 hours and 13 minutes.

St Martin's is the Gateway to the Fundy Trail. Visitors can drive the parkway following the cliffs, or hike the trail below.

LEFT: The oddly shaped cliffs, caves, flowerpots and arches are composed of red sandstone fused with rocks and pebbles from the 600-million-year-old Caledonia Mountain range. Once part of a valley floor, they were lifted during a period of tectonic activity and eroded into their present shapes over millions of years.

RIGHT: The site of some of the planet's highest tides, the Hopewell Rocks are one of the great marine wonders of the world. Here, you can walk on the ocean floor amid towering four-storey flowerpot rock formations and just a few hours later see them turn into tiny islands.

At Hopewell Rocks, visitors can venture out onto the red mudflats and essentially walk on the ocean floor. In summer, seabirds flock by the thousands to feed on the receding tide's buffet. Migrating sandpipers can double their weight in two to three weeks.

This abundance of food makes the Bay of Fundy one of the world's most enticing locations for hungry marine mammals. As many as 15 species of whales come to feast on the bountiful variety of food churned up by the region's powerful tides — more species than can be found at any time anywhere else.

LEFT: The Bay of Fundy's dramatic tides create extensive mudflats from thick deposits of red Triassic sandstone. Triassic fossils can sometimes be found in this muddy mixture.

141

47

MONTMORENCY FALLS
～ Quebec

L ocated at the mouth of the Montmorency River, about 11 kilometres (7 mi) northeast of Quebec City, Montmorency Falls plunge
83 metres (272 ft) into the waters of the St. Lawrence River, with
the Island of Orleans as a backdrop. The spectacular falls are as much as
30 metres (98 ft) higher than the far more famous Niagara Falls.

They were named for the duc de Montmorency, Henri II, viceroy of
New France from 1620 to 1625. Montmorency Falls played a historic role
when, during the Seven Years War, the Marquis de Montcalm and his
army fought off British General Wolfe's men here, taking the lives of 440
British troops, prior to Wolfe's successful surprise attack via the cliffs
below the Plains of Abraham. Ruins of British forts built in 1759 can be
seen in the eastern part of the park.

LEFT: In winter, spray from
the falls freezes into a several-
storeys-high mountain of ice
known locally as the *pain de
sucre* (sugarloaf).

LEFT: Montmorency Falls only
partly freeze. The basin carved
by the falls allows a continuous
flow behind an outer wall of
ice. Ice-climbing instruction is
available on site.

ABOVE: Located at the mouth of the Rivière Montmorency, Montmorency Falls are higher than world-famous Niagara Falls.

There are number of different viewing options. A cable-car service transports visitors to the top of the falls. An intricate set of 487 steps climbs the face of the gorge and offers several viewing platforms. There is also a suspension bridge across the crest of the falls.

The falls are illuminated at night throughout the summer, and a fireworks competition, Les Grands Feux Loto-Québec, is held here annually at the end of July. ✑

A suspension bridge over the crest of the falls allows access to boths sides of the park.

RIGHT: A stairway with 487 steps and numerous lookout points runs down the side of the gorge, offering many different views of the falls. If you don't feel like climbing 487 steep stairs, you can take the cable car to the top then descend via the stairway.

48

CALGARY STAMPEDE
∼ Alberta

The Calgary Stampede bills itself as the Greatest Outdoor Show on Earth. (Good-natured exaggeration is part of western culture.) It *is* a big event. More than 1,250,000 people attend the city's annual 10-day rodeo and exhibition.

It was big from the beginning. When American trick-roper Guy Weadick put together what he hoped would be a top-notch rodeo and Wild West show in 1912, he dreamed of cowboys coming from across North America to compete in a handful of events. Well, he got his cowboys. He also drew 100,000 spectators. In 1923, the Stampede combined forces with the annual Calgary Exhibition, and the two have been together ever since.

Chuckwagon racers compete for approximately $1 million in prize money, making this Stampede event the biggest of its kind. To put that in perspective, the 1923 chuckwagon race was the tenth event of the evening and had a combined purse of $275.

ABOVE: The Calgary Stampede hosts a full midway on its grounds, with over 50 rides and 70 carnival games. Concerts take place day and night in Stampede Park's outdoor amphitheatre, as well as at Nashville North and the famous Saddledome.

Whether or not it is the "greatest outdoor show," it remains the world's largest outdoor rodeo. Attendance at the annual Stampede Parade, which kicks off the 10-day celebration, averages about 350,000 people.

The rodeo itself features bareback competitions, bull-riding, ladies' barrel-racing, saddle-bronc riding, steer wrestling, tie-down roping, as well as novice bareback riding, novice saddle-bronc riding, junior steer-riding and wild pony-racing. A highlight is always the chuckwagon race, the Rangeland Derby, with top teams being put through their paces in a series of heats, each vying for the $100,000 awarded the winner of the final heat.

Other attractions include Aggie Days, a blacksmith competition, a team cattle-penning competition, a heavy horse show and pull, a vintage tractor pull, sheep show, cattle show, miniature donkey show, stock dog show, and the Acreage Lifestyle Show. A professional midway offers rides and carnival games, and concerts throughout Stampede Days feature top-name rock and country music acts. ⌒

RIGHT: Barrel-racing is the only women's event at the Stampede. Riders and their horses must circle three barrels in a cloverleaf pattern as fast as possible without knocking them over.

RIGHT: The First Nations people represented at the Stampede's Indian Village are from the Siksika, T'suu Tina, Nakoda (Stoney), Pikuni (Peigan) and Kainai (Blood) of Treaty 7. Over the ten days, the village hosts teepee-raising contests, powwows, Aboriginal music and dance performances, crafts demonstrations and much more.

49

TOP of the WORLD HIGHWAY
～ Yukon Territory

Y ou don't have to drive far west of Dawson City to understand why Yukon's Highway 9 is more colourfully known as the Top of the World Highway. For much of its length, it explores the crests of the steep hills and clings to rocky ridges well above treeline.

The highway connects West Dawson City with the Alaska border. The rest of Dawson is located on the east side of the Yukon River. The two are connected via ferry service or, in winter, over ice.

Top of the World Highway is only about 105 kilometres (66 mi) long, but what it lacks in length, it makes up for in height. The views down these alpine valleys are often breathtaking — as the road itself can be. You neither want to drive this road in an RV nor meet an RV coming the opposite direction. The highway is closed during winter months, when even snowmobilers are discouraged from using this route, mostly due to the fact that if a storm takes place, there is no shelter to be found. That's what it's like at the top of the world: great view but no place to hide.

It soon becomes obvious why this stretch of road between Dawson City and the Alaska border was given the name Top of the World Highway.

ABOVE: The border post is known as Little Gold Creek on the Canadian side and Poker Creek on the U.S. side, both names acknowledging the North's not-so-distant gold-rush history. If you're a nervous driver, you may think the Top of the World a bit of a gamble in spots, as well.

During summer, the Top of the World Highway provides motorists with a significant shortcut to Dawson City, a saving of about 800 kilometres (500 mi) over the alternate route through Whitehorse. This is true northern wilderness in all directions, and the transportation options pay tribute to that fact.

Shortly after crossing the U.S. border, the Top of the World connects with Alaska Route 5, the Taylor Highway, which leads either north to Eagle and south to Chicken. (The story goes that residents of the latter couldn't agree on the spelling of Ptarmigan.) Yes, they sell T-shirts. ∿

LEFT: At home in this northern wilderness, the snowy owl hunts for rodents in poorly drained freshwater meadows. More commonly seen are bear, moose, caribou and smaller animals such as Arctic fox, porcupine or the plentiful snowshoe hare.

50

GREAT SAND HILLS
～ Saskatchewan

If you didn't know better, on a mid-summer day you might think you were in the Sahara rather than Saskatchewan. The dunes are a surprising sight if you are accustomed to thinking of the Prairies as croplands and grain elevators. We usually associate sand dunes with our coastal regions, but the Great Sand Hills area is home to some of the largest and most active sand dunes in Canada.

The surrounding hills are simply sand dunes that have been stabilized by vegetation. This is a fragile ecosystem, and even the hills are highly subject to erosion. The stabilized areas support a wide range of vegetation, including indigenous prairie grasses, various cacti, creeping juniper, wild roses, saskatoon and chokecherry, and silver sagebrush.

Biologists have called the Great Sand Hills "an important genetic reservoir" for many Saskatchewan species.

Sandhill cranes are the most abundant of the world's cranes. They nest in low mounds built from local vegetation, and females usually lay two eggs. Both sexes incubate the eggs for approximately 30 days. Over 366 square kilometres (141 sq mi) in the Great Sand Hills were set aside as an ecological reserve in 2004. Sandhill cranes feel right at home here.

ABOVE: A dune is always a work-in-progress. Unanchored by vegetation, a large dune weighing many tons can "creep" up to 4 metres (13 ft) a year. One geologist reported examples of 19 dune types in the Great Sand Hills.

The hills are also home to white-tailed deer, antelopes, coyotes, badgers, weasels, porcupines, and even the Ord's kangaroo rat. Among highlights for birders are golden eagles, peregrine falcons, burrowing owls, white pelicans and, of course, sandhill cranes. ～

LEFT: The hills are a treasure-trove of wildlife. Sharp-tailed grouse are more abundant here than anywhere else in Canada, and the mule deer population is the densest in the province.

51

CAPE ST. MARY'S ECOLOGICAL RESERVE
～ Newfoundland

Birdwatchers will find Cape St. Mary's Ecological Reserve one of the most accessible and spectacular seabird rookeries in the world.

Located at the tip of the southwestern arm of Newfoundland's Avalon Peninsula, during breeding season it is home to tens of thousands of northern gannets, black-legged kittiwakes and common murres. Lesser numbers of thick-billed murres, razorbills, black guillemots, double-crested and great cormorants, and northern fulmars also nest here. In addition, the reserve supports a seaduck population that includes oldsquaw, scoters, eiders and even the endangered harlequin duck. ～

BELOW: Most of the area's northern gannets choose to nest on Bird Rock, a 100-metre (328 ft) sandstone sea stack. Visitors can view the nesting birds from rock ledges just a short distance away.

ABOVE: Northern gannets are the largest seabirds in the North Atlantic. The female lays a single large white egg in a nest of dried seaweed in early June. The chick hatches in July, and by September, they are on their way south for the winter.

Perhaps the main attraction is Bird Rock, reached by a 1-kilometre (half-mile) trail through an open meadow that tops steep cliffs. This is one of the world's most southerly expanses of sub-Arctic tundra. Low-lying shrubs and wildflowers carpet the ground. Some of the algae found on rocks atop this plateau have been found to be millions of years old.

The striking-looking northern gannets put on the most elaborate show with their courtship, nesting, and feeding rituals. They began nesting on Bird Rock in the late nineteenth century, when they discovered that it offered protection from terrestrial predators. ☙

RIGHT: Sheep graze in the meadows atop the high cliffs. While they may brave the edges, visitors should beware. Damp grass, sheep manure and bird droppings can make for slippery footing.

52

BEACHCOMBING
by HELICOPTER
~ British Columbia

Beachcombing is always a relaxing activity. Beachcombing by helicopter is, conversely, a thrilling activity.

Many of the same BC tour companies that offer upscale fishing and wildlife-viewing trips also offer helicopter beachcombing trips. Hard-to-reach beaches hold the lion's share of beachcombing treasure, and it's a singular experience having a stretch of sand and surf to one's self.

Vancouver, the Sunshine Coast, Vancouver Island, the Gulf Islands, the Queen Charlottes, the Caribou Chilcotin Coast — just about every coastal region, park and community claims to be great for beachcombing. But a knowledgeable helicopter pilot can take you to secluded coves and hidden beaches that may not have seen humans for months or even years.

Many of the tour companies that offer executive fishing trips and whale-watching trips also offer spectacular helicopter beachcombing excursions.

You can find bleached whale bones, sperm whale teeth, crabs, clams, mussels, periwinkles, cockle shells, limpet shells, scallop shells, sand dollars, unusual rocks and driftwood formations. You can also find coins, cans, jars, bottles, crates. And then there are the more bizarre finds. In 1990 a shipping container containing some 80,000 Nike running shoes toppled into the sea and began washing ashore in the Pacific Northwest. Beachcombers combined forces to match up pairs. More recently, a similar tactical mission was organized to deal with beached hockey gloves.

As seasoned beachcombers will tell you, beachcombing isn't about what you find, it's about looking closely at what might otherwise be taken for granted. It's about being in the moment, in a beautiful place. There are seemingly endless beautiful places to be discovered along this province's shorelines.

ABOVE: Travel by helicopter is a great way to see the epic coastline of British Columbia and the fastest way to reach magnificent out-of-the-way locations.

LEFT: It's not unusual to discover unbroken glass floats used in Japanese fishing nets or all manner of beautiful shells. There are, however, bigger items to be found.

BELOW: There is something inexplicably soothing about the look of rounded pebbles washed by the tide.

53

MORAINE LAKE and the VALLEY of TEN PEAKS
~ Alberta

LEFT: Rockpile Trail offers the most photographed view of the lake and peaks, but there is another trailhead near the canoe docks of Moraine Lake Lodge. Two trails start here, one of them branching into four more trails, five trails in total: Moraine Lake Lakeshore Trail, Eiffel Lake, Wenkchemna Pass, Larch Valley and Sentinel Pass.

BELOW: Moraine Lake turns a vivid turquoise when it crests in mid-June. This is due to fine particles of glacial silt known as rock flour. Light refracts off of the rock flour, creating intense colour.

Situated in the Valley of Ten Peaks, at an elevation of approximately 1884 metres (6,183 ft), Moraine Lake is a sister lake to Lake Louise. Many will recognize it from the back of a 1970s Canadian $20 bill. It is considered by many to be one of the most scenic lakes in the Canadian Rockies.

In the nineteenth-century, visiting mountaineers honoured their Stoney guides by naming the ten peaks using numbers from the Stoney language: Heejee, Nom, Yamnee, Tonsa, Sapta, Shappee, Sagowa, Saknowa, Neptuak and Wenkchemna. Only Sapta, Neptuak and Wenkchemna still retain their Native names.

To get the best view of the peaks and the lake, hike the Rockpile Trail to the top of the large rockpile at the lake's outlet. The highest of the Ten Peaks is Deltaform Mountain (Saknowa until 1897), at 3424 metres (11,234 ft). Three additional peaks can be seen from here: Mt. Temple, Mt. Babel and Eiffel Peak. The huge mountain to the north with the glacier on its summit is Mt. Temple, the third highest mountain in the park. The Continental Divide runs across the ragged peaks behind the lake.

The area around the lake offers several hiking trails, with occasional restrictions due to grizzly bear activity. It's more common to see elk, moose and bighorn sheep. ~

54 CONFEDERATION BRIDGE
～ Prince Edward Island

The slogan for Prince Edward Island's Confederation Bridge is "The longest bridge. The shortest route."

Potential ways of linking Prince Edward Island and mainland Canada have been discussed almost since the province entered confederation in 1873. The first ferry service across the Northumberland Strait began in 1917, and for the next 80 years the island was accessible only by ferry or aircraft.

In October 1993 the Government of Canada signed an agreement with a consortium of Canadian enterprises, to finance, build, operate and maintain a bridge connecting Prince Edward Island to the mainland. The new Confederation Bridge opened on May 31, 1997.

The first submarine telegraph cable in British North America was laid along the sea floor between the same two points of land in 1851.

Some 310 streetlights illuminate the bridge, and closed-circuit television cameras are positioned at regular intervals to monitor activity at all times.

ABOVE: and BELOW: Confederation Bridge is divided into three parts: West Approach, East Approach and the Main Bridge. The Main Bridge rests on 44 piers and stands 60 metres (197 ft) above water at its highest point.

The 12.9-kilometre (8 mi) bridge joins Borden-Carleton, Prince Edward Island, and Cape Jourimain, New Brunswick, and is the longest bridge over ice-covered waters in the world. It is an engineering marvel.

The bridge carries two lanes of traffic at an average height of 40 metres (131 ft) above water. It remains open 24 hours a day, 7 days a week, and is closed only in the most extreme weather. Some 7,300 drain ports handle the runoff of rainwater and melting snow and ice.

One hundred and twenty-four years after Prince Edward Island joined the rest of Canada, it became joined *to* the rest of Canada, changing commerce and travel between islanders and mainlanders forever. ⌇

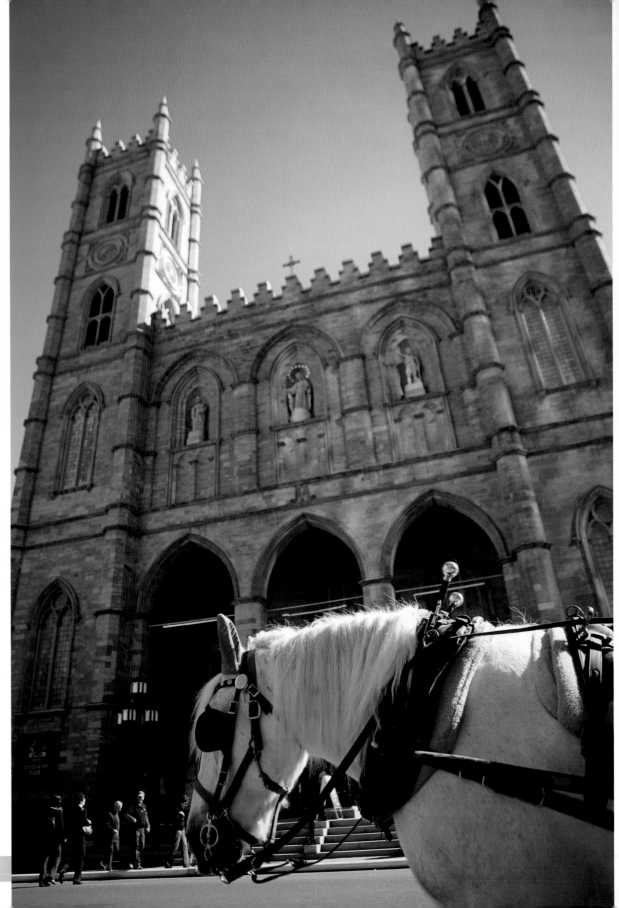

55

OLD MONTREAL
⁓ Quebec

LEFT: Notre-Dame Basilica is an Old Montreal landmark. Its exterior is Gothic Revival in design, while its sanctuary features rich hues of red, purple, silver and gold. Stained-glass windows depict scenes from the city's religious history. Its Canadian-built organ is one of the largest in the world, with almost 7,000 pipes.

Montreal has one of the oldest city centres in North America. Some of its buildings date as far back as the late 1600s, and granite paving stones along streets, sidewalks and in public spaces mark the buried remains of the once fortified city's stone walls and main structures.

The city was founded as a missionary colony by Paul de Chomedey de Maisonneuve in 1642, but the burgeoning business of fur trading — and resultant territorial hostilities with the Iroquois — soon took priority. Wooden fortifications were built almost immediately, and Louis XIV approved construction of a stone fortification in 1712. By mid-century, Montreal was a French village tucked away within fortified stone walls. Anyone with business in the village had to pass through the gates of the fort.

But prospering, bilingual Montreal inevitably saw the arrival of tens of thousands of immigrants from Europe and the British Isles, and beginning in 1804 its historic fortifications were torn down to facilitate the first of many waves of urban expansion.

BELOW: You can hire a horse-drawn calèche and driver for a wonderful tour down Rue Saint-Paul and the side streets of the Old Port. Drivers must have a thorough knowledge of the district's history and architecture to receive licensing.

ABOVE: The Old Port of Montreal has been a hub of activity since the early 1600s. Today, it welcomes over seven million visitors a year to its quays.

The revival of Old Montreal as the artistic and cultural hub of the city began in the 1960s. Over the next couple of decades, architects restored many of its historic buildings and homes, and city planners acknowledged the heritage and tourism value of a bustling city centre then well into its fourth century.

Today, the Old Montreal area is home to six major museums, the Montreal Science Centre, the Montreal World Trade Centre, City Hall, the famous Bonsecours Market, Notre-Dame Basilica, vestiges of the city's original fortifications at Champ-de-Mars, historic Place d'Armes, Place Royale and Place Jacques-Cartier, dozens of boutiques, restaurants and cafes, street displays by artists and craftspeople on Saint-Amable and Saint-Vincent, and the daily activities of the Old Port.

Montreal celebrated its 365th birthday in 2007, and it continues to be a modern New World city with a decidedly Old World charm. ⌁

ABOVE and RIGHT: The narrow cobblestone streets of Old Montreal give it an Old World European feel that is further reflected in its many museums, galleries, cafés and boutiques. The domed Bonsecours Market building houses the Conseil des métiers d'art du Québec and Institute of Design Montréal, as well as award-winning restaurants and 15 boutiques.

56

The FORTRESS of LOUISBOURG
∼ Nova Scotia

LEFT: Each summer, costumed actors of all ages portray Louisbourg life as it might have been in the summer of 1744. Each role was meticulously researched, and each actor carries out his or her role with uncanny authenticity

BELOW: Visit the home of Étienne Verrier, the King's engineer, to learn about the village's layout, its key buildings and fortifications, and the engineer's duties during time of siege.

T he Fortress of Louisbourg is a reconstructed eighteenth-century fortified French village. As you make your way around, you have to remind yourself that it has been *reconstructed*. Everything in the village has been painstakingly recreated based on artifacts from local archaeological excavations and period documents held in archives in France, England, Scotland, the United States and Canada.

After losing Newfoundland and Acadia to the British under the Treaty of Utrecht in 1713, France held only Isle Royale and Isle Saint-Jean (Cape Breton and Prince Edward Island) in what would become Atlantic Canada. Louisbourg was the capital of Isle Royale and prospered with the thriving Grand Banks cod fishery and trade in goods imported from France, the West Indies and New England.

British troops took Louisbourg in 1745 and again in 1758. Each time, it required almost seven weeks of battle. To prevent such resistance from occurring a third time, the British demolished the fortress walls.

A $25-million Government of Canada project begun in 1961 has seen nearly a quarter of the original settlement accurately restored to its pre-1745 condition. The Fortress of Louisbourg is operated by Parks Canada as a National Historic Site.

"Residents" of the fortress re-enact the daily lives of fishermen and merchants; the family life of a working soldier; and the more privileged life of Captain and Madame DeGannes. Minstrels sing, dance and tell stories, while other villagers demonstrate such activities as blacksmithing, gardening, open-hearth cooking and lace-making.

57

DAWSON CITY
～ Yukon

Dawson is Gold Rush City. When word of the Klondike gold discovery reached U.S. newspapers in 1897, some 100,000 people headed north to try their luck. Dawson is said to have been laid out in a grid pattern on a moose pasture, but it would become, for brief but gilded moments, one of the liveliest cities on the continent.

While most new arrivals continued on to the gold fields, pick and pan in hand, others saw the boom in terms of more traditional business opportunities and set up dry goods and hardware stores, outfitting establishments, eateries, saloons and dance halls. Gambling and prostitution were tolerated, but otherwise the North West Mounted Police kept a lawful community, contrary to the scandalous tales written by dime novelists of the day.

Located in a building constructed in 1904, Klondike Kate's Cabins & Restaurant is named for Kathleen "Klondike Kate" Rockwell. Born in Kansas, she came to Dawson as a "vivacious and popular" entertainer. Kate died in 1957, at age 80, and her ghost is said to still haunt an upstairs dressing room in the Palace Grand.

LEFT: Buildings were given false fronts to make them appear grander, but behind the façade, most were of simple log construction.

BELOW: Between June and September 1898, 57 registered steamboats with 12,000 tons of supplies docked at Dawson City. A year later, 60 steamboats, 8 tugs and 20 barges were in service on the river.

The new town of Dawson, located at the mouth of the Klondike River, soon boasted a floating-but-steady population of 30,000, making it the largest city north of Seattle.

Some of the early Gold Rush buildings were constructed using as floors the same flat-bottomed boats that had carried their owners upriver.

Many of the city's major buildings are part of Dawson National Historic Site and feature colourful displays as well as Parks employees dressed in Klondike costume. Diamond Tooth Gertie's Gambling Hall, Canada's first and most northerly casino, offers nightly can-can shows. Other attractions include the Jack London Interpretive Centre, Berton House, Robert Service's cabin, the S.S. *Keno* National Historic Site, and the Dawson City Museum.

58

ILE BONAVENTURE
and PERCÉ ROCK
~ Quebec

The Gaspé Peninsula and Gulf of St. Lawrence region attracts tourists with its spectacular scenery, but for 280,000 migrating seabirds, it's all about the sex. Well, more precisely, the elaborate breeding rituals, the nesting, the brief rearing of offspring, and the weeks of glutinous pre-departure feeding.

Bonaventure Island and Percé Rock National Park is one of the world's largest and most accessible bird sanctuaries. Bonaventure hosts North America's largest nesting colony of northern gannets, tens of thousands of nesting pairs, as well as black-legged kittiwakes, murres, terns, black guillemots, auks, razorbills, gulls, cormorants, puffins, and many other species. Over 290 species have been logged by birders at one time or another.

RIGHT: Bonaventure Island lies approximately 3.5 kilometres (2 mi) off the southeast coast of the Gaspé Peninsula. It became a migratory bird sanctuary in 1919 and a national park in 1985.

BELOW: Each year, a colony of approximately 100,000 gannets nests in Bonaventure Island and Percé Rock National Park in the Gaspé region of Quebec. Bonaventure Island is home to North America's largest nesting colony of northern gannets.

ABOVE and OPPOSITE: Rocher Percé, "pierced rock," is one of the world's largest and most recognizable natural arches. The arch is some 15 metres (50 ft) high. The massive limestone stack had two arches until the outer one broke free and collapsed on June 17, 1845.

LEFT: Visitors can walk out to Percé Rock during low tide. It is one of the most popular natural-landform destinations in Quebec. The rock contains millions of marine fossils from the Devonian period, 415 to 360 million years ago.

Samuel de Champlain saw the towering limestone stack in 1603 and named it "Rocher Percé." More than 400 years later, CBC Radio listeners have nominated it as one of the Seven Wonders of Canada.

From May to October, boat and island tours operate out of the town of Percé, taking visitors past Bonaventure Island's picturesque cliffs and beaches (and countless thousands of seabirds) before docking trailside. Four intersecting trails lead to the nesting colonies. Be forewarned that this is nature at its noisiest: clacking, scraping, squawking, cawing, shrieking, beckoning and threatening.

The walk from the mainland to Percé Rock at low tide begins at the parking lot on Mont-Joli. This impressive limestone stack is 433 metres (1,420 ft) long, 90 metres (296 ft) wide and 88 metres (289 ft) at its highest point. It is perhaps the most photographed feature on the Gaspé Peninsula. According to local legend, nineteenth-century villagers climbed to its summit each harvest season to collect the three tons of hay growing there. ～

59

The ROCKY MOUNTAINEER TRAIN TRIP
∼ Alberta & British Columbia

LEFT and FOLLOWING PAGES: The *Mountaineer* winds its way past snow-capped peaks, escarpments, glaciers, pine forests, pea-cock-blue lakes, rushing waterfalls, through valleys, canyons and even the high desert of the Okanagan.

There really is no better way to see the Canadian Rockies than aboard the *Rocky Mountaineer*. It's a two-day, all-daylight journey departing from Banff, Calgary or Jasper and ending at the grand Rocky Mountaineer Station in Vancouver.

During those two days, you will cross five mountain ranges, travel past high desert and temperate rainforest, and terminate alongside the Pacific Ocean. Various travel packages extend the experience with side trips to national parks and hot springs, and for motorcoach tours, glacier helicopter tours, mountain gondola and icefield explorer rides, and overnight stays in several top hotels, including the famous Fairmont Chateau Lake Louise.

BELOW: *Rocky Mountaineer* RedLeaf service offers passengers large picture-window views of the mountains' incredible vistas. GoldLeaf service offers luxury seating in domed cars, placing passengers in the wilderness while they enjoy every comfort.

ABOVE: The *Rocky Mountaineer* travels only during daylight hours, so you won't miss a thing.

With an average speed of 50 kilometres per hour (30 mph), wildlife sightings are common, with wapiti, bison, bighorn sheep, mountain goats, elk, caribou and bears the most visible. Eagles and hawks roam the skies, and osprey nest atop trees, outcrops and telephone poles.

The highest point of the trip is the Continental Divide at 1,625 metres (5,332 ft). Canadian and provincial flags mark the Divide. The *Mountaineer* navigates some of the steeper grades through spiral tunnels. A stretch along the Columbia River almost challenges amateur photographers to try their luck at capturing a place so beautiful in a framed image.

With the glamorous GoldLeaf service, a 45-person staff attends to your every need. They also provide a running commentary on the area's history, geology, flora, and fauna.

GoldLeaf service also offers meals based on regional cuisine, prepared by onboard gourmet chefs.

60

SKATING on the RIDEAU CANAL
~ Ontario

Each winter Ottawa's section of the Rideau Canal becomes the world's largest skating rink. The "Skateway" holds the Guinness World Record for the World's Largest Naturally Frozen Ice Rink, with a groomed ice surface equal to some 100 regulation hockey rinks placed end to end.

Skating season on the canal usually begins in late December and runs until early March. It is open for public use daily, as weather permits. A flag system is used to signal ice conditions: a red flag means it is closed to skating; yellow means conditions are fair to good; and green means very good to excellent.

The Skateway winds through downtown Ottawa and handles an average of one million skaters per season. Many enjoy a quiet, less crowded moonlight skate.

LEFT: Ottawa is a city that embraces winter, and many central Canadians take short, rejuvenating winter holidays to the nation's capital, always including skating sessions on the canal. Hardy locals skate to work or school whenever weather permits.

BELOW: Canada's National Capital Region hosts Winterlude each February. One of the highlights is the International Ice Carving Competition that takes place in Confederation Park.

Once cold-weather conditions have established a good ice base on the canal, crews maintain the surface by pumping water onto it overnight to create a fresh layer of smooth ice for the next day's skaters.

While most of North America celebrates warm weather, Ottawa's thousands of skaters know that a brisk cold snap means great ice.

Skating is free, with donations welcome. With public safety in mind, dogs, bicycles and hockey sticks are not allowed on ice surface.

It's a wonderful and surprisingly uplifting thing to be on the ice on a sunny day in the nation's capital city with people of all ages, all cultures, all levels of skating ability, all smiles. It's seems deeply Canadian.

Ottawa's popular winter festival, Winterlude, occurs over the first three weekends in February. Its attractions include international ice and snow sculpting competitions, the world's largest snow playground, and a variety of multicultural events.

61

CAPE BONAVISTA
∼ Newfoundland

LEFT: The Bonavista Peninsula separates Bonavista Bay (north) from Trinity Bay (south). This is a rugged point of land that often experiences the fury of the North Atlantic. Despite it's wild beauty, one can imagine the life of an isolated nineteenth-century lightkeeper on these rocks.

BELOW: Each year thousands of visitors take guided tours of the light at Cape Bonavista. Interpreters dressed in circa-1870 costume tell of the hard life of the lightkeepers who maintained the light. From roughly April through July, icebergs and whales can be seen just off the cape.

The story goes that John Cabot left Bristol, England, aboard his ship the *Matthew* in May 1497 and sighted land at what is now Cape Bonavista on June 24. It's said that upon reaching the Grand Banks, the captain and crew encountered cod so thick that they slowed the ship's progress. Cabot is thought to have been born in Genoa, Italy, and the name Bonavista may be derived from the Italian *O buon vista* ("Oh, happy sight").

Cape Bonavista is the rocky tip of the Bonavista Peninsula, just north of the town of Bonavista. It offers a wind-whipped, breathtaking, wave-crashing view of the Atlantic, but most people come to see the lighthouse.

One of Newfoundland's earliest lighthouses was built here in 1843 to guide mariners around the rocky peninsula. The lantern was supported by a two-storey stone tower inside a wood frame. The original lantern came from Inchcape (Bell) Rock lighthouse in Scotland. In 1895 that was replaced by another Scottish light. The lighthouse was converted to electricity in 1962. The electric light was placed on a metal tower outside the building in 1966, and the 1895 catoptric apparatus was returned to the lighthouse.

The lighthouse living quarters have been furnished with pre-1870 furniture and artifacts similar to those that would have been used when 80-year-old Jeremiah White was still lightkeeper, with the help of his son Nicholas, the assistant keeper, and his family. ∼

The original lantern came from Inchcape (Bell) Rock lighthouse in Scotland.

62 VANCOUVER SEAWALL
~ British Columbia

Few of the world's major cities are so perfectly nestled amid ocean, beaches and mountains. Though densely populated, Vancouver offers its residents and visitors near instant access to nature.

The Stanley Park Seawall and its extension, the West Vancouver Seawall, provide extraordinary views of green parklands, the Pacific Ocean and local landmark Lions Gate Bridge. For Vancouverites, the seawall is an ever-present oasis just minutes from hectic urban life.

ABOVE: Lions Gate Bridge connects North and West Vancouver with Stanley Park and the City of Vancouver. Wide sidewalks allow pedestrians to walk or jog across the bridge.

LEFT: After years of extensions, the Stanley Park Seawall is only one part of the world's longest unbroken urban waterfront walkway.

RIGHT: Inspired by Copenhagen's famous mermaid, the life-sized bronze statue *Girl in a Wetsuit* is said to represent Vancouver's dependence on the sea. It is the work of sculptor Elek Imredy and is located on a boulder just off the northern shore of Stanley Park.

ABOVE: Scottish master stonemason James Cunningham made the seawall his life's work. Cunningham coordinated construction of the granite and concrete wall for 32 years, until he was in his 80s. The memorial James Cunningham Seawall Race is held on the last Sunday of October.

The West Vancouver Seawall starts in beautiful Ambleside village and continues to the charming, boutique-lined community of Dundarave. The "Seawalk," as it is sometimes called, looks directly across the inlet to Stanley Park and the Vancouver skyline.

Across the Lions Gate Bridge, the famous Stanley Park Seawall proceeds to encircle Canada's largest city park, offering stunning views of the North Shore mountains. A complete circumnavigation of Stanley Park takes about two hours at a brisk pace.

At various times of day, you'll encounter tai chi practitioners, runners, race-walkers, cyclists, inline skaters, people out for a leisurely stroll, and hand-holding romantics. Overall, a healthy, positive-minded swath of humanity. Even the safety monitors, the Seawall Skate Patrol, travel the route on inline skates. ⌣

63

GLACIER LAKE
～ Northwest Territories

ABOVE: Access is by floatplane or via the South Nahanni River — Glacier Lake Trail, a 20-kilometre (12.4-mi) trek with the difficulty rating "high." The Parks service advises against portaging canoes and heavy gear along this route. Public-use canoes are available on the shore of Glacier Lake.

LEFT: Glacier Lake is located at the entrance to the Cirque of the Unclimbables, a collection of steep-faced peaks known to climbers worldwide.

BELOW: Glacier Lake and the South Nahanni River as seen from the Ragged Range.

You get here by floatplane or via the South Nahanni River–Glacier Lake Trail, a relatively difficult wilderness hike best suited to those with backcountry experience. However you get here, it's worth the effort.

Located to the north of Nahanni National Park Reserve, Glacier Lake offers breathtaking views in every direction from its site at the entrance to the Ragged Range and the famous Cirque of the Unclimbables.

In the 1930s, a man named Harry Snyder came here to "collect" taxidermied examples of a rare species of mountain sheep for the National Museum of Canada and the American Museum of Natural History. The government decided to rescind permission when it learned that Snyder had begun construction of a hunting lodge along Glacier Lake. Because of Harry, Glacier Lake became a game preserve.

Snyder turned his attention to endangered wood bison and led a "collection" expedition in Wood Buffalo National Park. It took three trips to fill all his museum orders. He also requested, and was denied, permission to hunt endangered muskox in the Thelon district. Snyder redeemed himself somewhat by funding aerial surveys of muskox populations and their ranges.

When Harry died at his ranch northwest of Calgary, the house was said to be full of rare books and paintings, stuffed animals from around the world, and Dene and Inuit artifacts rivaling those held in the world's best museum collections. ～

64 MAGDALEN ISLANDS SEALS, BIRDS & SANDCASTLES
～ Quebec

The Magdalen Islands (Îles de la Madeleine in French) are located 215 kilometres (134 mi) off the Gaspé Peninsula, in the Gulf of St. Lawrence. Though part of the province of Quebec, they are geographically closer to Cape Breton and Prince Edward Island.

The archipelago consists of approximately a dozen islands, six of which are connected by narrow sand dunes. The islands' rocky outcrops are linked by sand spits, which are endlessly reshaped by the unimpeded winds. Dunes called *buttereaux* have been known to reach up to 15 metres (49 ft) in height.

The Magdalens offer many attractions, including gourmet tours, historical and architectural excursions, lighthouse visits, music festivals, arts and crafts fairs, kayaking, windsurfing, kite-surfing, sailing, diving, snorkeling, cycling, but among the most popular are seal-watching, Bird Rock tours and the annual sandcastle competition.

BELOW: Until the twentieth century, residents of the Magdalen Islands were isolated during the winter, as pack ice (large chunks of floating drift ice driven together) made boat travel to and from the mainland impossible.

ABOVE: Several tour companies offer helicopter trips to observe the seals in their natural habitat. Harp seal pups grow at an amazing rate and are able to be weaned approximately two weeks after birth. During these two weeks, the young lose their white coats and become *guenilloux* ("ragged-jackets").

Four different species of seal can be found in the islands. Grey seals and harbour seals can be seen and photographed in their natural surroundings from the deck of a tour boat. For those who want a closer look, Zodiac tours are available, with the chance to snorkel among the seal herd living near Corps-Mort Rock.

LEFT: The harp seal migrates from the Arctic to the coast of Newfoundland and the Magdalen Islands near the end of December. Birthing of new pups occurs at the beginning of March, when hundreds of thousands of harp seals come to the ice floes around the Islands to calve the "whitecoats."

ABOVE: Bird Rock, Entry Island and Brion Island are among the best seabird colony observation sites in the Magdalens.

Birdwatchers will find many additions to their life list in the meadows, marches, ponds, dunes and tidal zones, but for the full nesting-colony experience, take a trip to Bird Rock, where throughout the summer the northern gannet, black-legged kittiwake, great blue heron, double-crested cormorant, black guillemot, Atlantic puffin, razorbill and other seabirds breed, rear their young and fatten themselves for the long flight south. Endangered species such as the piping plover, roseate tern and horned grebe may also be seen, but should not be disturbed. Migratory shorebirds include sandpipers, plovers, yellowlegs, turnstones, whimbrels and Hudsonian godwits.

RIGHT: There are only about 25 resident bird species on the islands, but some 200 species of seabirds, shorebirds and waterfowl visit annually. The endangered piping plover nests on the islands' beaches and is found nowhere else in Quebec

Unlike many sand-sculpture competitions, this one requires that the creation represent a castle. Entries in the adult category must be at least 1 metre (39 in) high.

The Sandcastle Contest takes place on the beach in Havre-Aubert, Îles-de-la-Madeleine, during the second weekend of August. Sand-castle-building workshops are offered in the weeks prior to the contest.

The Magdalens enjoy a mild climate, with warm breezes and plenty of sunshine, which is perfect for the popular Concours de Châteaux de sable (Sandcastle Contest). The contest takes place on the beach in Havre-Aubert during the second weekend of August. ∾

65

WRITING-ON-STONE PROVINCIAL PARK
~ Alberta

Writing-on-Stone Provincial Park contains the largest concentration of petroglyphs on the North American Plains and is designated as a National Historic Site. It is also one of the largest areas of protected prairie in Alberta, preserving significant coulee and prairie wildlife habitats and home to a reconstructed North West Mounted Police outpost that depicts the area's role in bringing law and order to the Canadian West.

Petroglyphs (rock carvings) and pictographs (rock paintings) are part of an ancient tradition of aboriginal rock art. Some of the earliest art at Writing-on-Stone may be as much as 5,000 years old and was probably carved by the Shoshoni, Sioux, Assiniboine and Gros Ventre people.

In the mid-1700s members of the Blackfoot Confederation came to the land. The Blackfoot people still consider the land here sacred, and through exhibits and programs in the new Áísínai'pi Visitor Centre they hope to portray the rich history of the area's First Nations.

The rock art was generally used to depict important life events. It also played a ceremonial role, and some of it may constitute a record of vision-quest dreams. The petroglyphs were made by using pieces of bone, horn or rock to gouge images into the sandstone. The pictographs were painted using ochre, a mixture of crushed iron ore and animal fat that produced red, yellow and orange colours.

Park staff and members of the Blood Tribe of the Blackfoot Nation work together to help visitors experience the historic, cultural and spiritual importance of this ancient place. ~

RIGHT: Pictures were etched into the sandstone's surface with tools made from bone, horn or harder rock. The events depicted were significant hunts or battles.

BELOW: Archaeological evidence shows that people camped here for at least 3,500 years. The land provided them with sufficient food, water and shelter, and interpretations of the writings suggest that supernatural powers were believed to inhabit the sandstone cliffs and hoodoo rock formations.

66

MT. LOGAN
~ Yukon

Mount Logan is the highest elevation in Canada. Located in the St. Elias Mountains, in Kluane National Park, in the southwestern Yukon, near the Alaska border, it stands 5959 metres (19,551 ft) high. Or it did a minute ago. Due to ongoing tectonic activity, Mount Logan is still rising in elevation.

Logan is not only the highest peak in Canada, it is the second highest in North America, one of the most massive in the world, and has the largest base circumference of any mountain on Earth. The Logan massif extends about 3000 metres (9,843 ft) above the surrounding glaciers. One climber explained it this way: "To put it in perspective, the Zermatt would nicely fill in the summit plateau, or you take the entire High Peaks Region of the Adirondacks, or if you like you can take Mont Blanc and Kilimanjaro, put them on the plateau, and there would still be room left for the Eiger."

Logan's many cliff faces, some of them well over 3050 metres (10,000 ft), rise to form an immense 16-kilometre-long (10 mi) crest of peaks, sub-peaks and saddles, while its huge, heavily crevassed glaciers spill into the surrounding valleys.

It's big and it's hard to reach, making it the object of many a mountaineer's desires. Mount Logan has been described as "more spectacular than Mount McKinley and without the crowds." It has become a bit of a cliché to call a location "one of the last wild places on Earth," but to even *see* Logan necessitates a tough two-day hike from the nearest trailhead. ~

RIGHT: Logan's summit protrudes from the world's largest ice sheet that is not part of an ice cap. The heavily crevassed glaciers atop the summit plateau spill down into the surrounding valleys.

BELOW: Canada's highest peak, Mount Logan is part of a glaciated plateau, with numerous ridges leading up to it and about a dozen peaks rising from it, the highest being Logan's main summit. The mountain was named for Sir William Logan, founder of the Geological Survey of Canada.

67

GWAII HAANAS
NATIONAL PARK RESERVE
~ British Columbia

Gwaii Haanas — "islands of the people" — is the Haida name for the Queen Charlotte Islands. According to Haida legend, this is the place where time began.

If not where time began, these islands do seem like a world unto themselves. And they were for the Haida, whose connection to this land and the surrounding sea goes back 10,000 years.

There are 1,884 islands in the Gwaii Haanas archipelago. The seven largest islands, north to south, are Langara, Graham, Moresby, Louise, Lyell, Burnaby and Kunghit. They are managed jointly by the Government of Canada and the Council of the Haida Nation under a unique agreement. While the two parties disagree as to ownership, they strongly agree on the need to protect the land, marine habitat and cultural heritage of Gwaii Haanas.

ABOVE: Many common mainland species have evolved into unique Gwaii Haanas subspecies. The black bear and the pine marten, for instance, are both larger than their mainland cousins

BELOW: The San Christoval Mountains form the backbone of Gwaii Haanas, rising to 1123 metres (3,684 ft) at Mount de la Touche. The 50-kilometre (31 mi) mountain range is located on the west coast of Moresby Island. Moresby and Graham islands comprise the largest landmass in the 1,884-island Queen Charlottes.

ABOVE: Just west of the islands, the continental shelf falls away dramatically. Movement by the tectonic plates below the ocean floor make this paradise the most active earthquake area in Canada.

The islands' unusual and abundant plant and animal species have earned Gwaii Haanas the nickname "Galapagos of the North." Species here often differ from those found on the mainland. Many common continental species are not found on the islands, and some that are have evolved into unique subspecies.

The ocean here teems with salmon, herring, halibut, rockfish, mussels, crab, starfish, sea urchin and octopus. Grey, orca, humpback and minke whales can be seen, as well as dolphins, porpoises and harbour seals.

Haida watchmen live at camps at the old village sites of K'uuna Llnagaay (Skedans), T'aanuu Llnagaay (Tanu), Hlk'yah GaawGa (Windy Bay), Gandll K'in Gwaayaay (Hotspring Island) and SGang Gwaay (Anthony Island), ensuring that these sites are respected. The watchmen generously share their knowledge with visitors.

Gwaii Haanas National Park Reserve includes the ancient and now abandoned Haida village site of Ninstints on Anthony Island. Ninstints village was designated a UNESCO World Heritage Site in 1981 in recognition of its cultural value and importance to the history of mankind.

The weathered, decaying "Ninstints" totem poles of SGang Gwaay speak of a sad period in Haida history. (Fur traders derived the name Ninstints from a corruption of then-chief Nan Sdins' name.) In the 1800s, contact with Europeans and their foreign diseases decimated populations in several main Haida villages. At the time, SGang Gwaay was the most important village in the Haida realm. Today, it is a silent village watched over by ancient totems, protected by Haida watchmen, honoured as a UNESCO World Heritage Site, and a deeply spiritual destination to all who visit.

68

KILLARNEY & LA CLOCHE MOUNTAINS
~ Ontario

LEFT: Legend has it that the white quartzite rocks of the La Cloche Mountains were used by the Natives as *tocsins* (warning bells). When struck like a bell, the sound could be heard for a great distance. The French word for bell is *la Cloche*.

BELOW: Killarney is a vast and beautiful wilderness, with pristine lakes, distinctive white quartzite ridges, and transition-zone forests of pine and hardwood. It has long been a favourite destination for artists, including the Group of Seven's A.Y. Jackson.

Killarney Provincial Park's white quartzite La Cloche Mountains were formed some two billion years ago and once stood higher than the present-day Rocky Mountains. Today, they are more like massive, rounded stone hills that mountain peaks. Over the past million years or so, four ice ages have scraped away the mountaintops, leaving the rocky ridges that now dominate the landscape.

Though they may lack their former glory, the La Cloche Mountains' distinctive appearance has attracted artists and writers, canoeists and hikers for decades. In fact, it was due to a lobby by artists, including A.Y. Jackson, that the Ontario government made Killarney a provincial park.

The park lies in the transition zone between northern boreal forest and the St. Lawrence–Great Lakes lowlands, providing habitat for an unusually diverse range of plants and animals. Mammals include typical northern species such as moose, deer, wolves, bobcat, marten and beaver, but over 20 species of reptiles and amphibians can also be found in the park.

Killarney offers 140 backcountry canoe-in sites and 33 backcountry hike-in sites. The La Cloche Silhouette Trail is a magnificent but challenging 100-kilometre (60-mi) loop that takes 7-10 days to complete. Much of the park is accessible year-round, and it is a popular destination for cross-country skiers and snowshoers in the winter. ~

69

ICEFIELDS PARKWAY
~ Alberta

The 230-kilometre (142-mi) Icefields Parkway connects Lake Louise to Jasper via the heart of the Rockies. Its snow-capped peaks, massive glaciers, turquoise lakes, vibrant wildflower meadows and dense forests make it one of the world's great scenic drives.

Construction began in the early 1930s as part of an unemployment relief project. The road was finally opened to motorists in 1940 and was upgraded in the 1960s. Though dwarfed by its grand surroundings, it is a generously proportioned two-lane highway with relatively easy grades and paved shoulders that allow passing and room for cyclists.

The route links the valleys of the Bow, Mistaya, North Saskatchewan, Sunwapta, and Athabasca rivers, and features spectacular views of some of the highest mountains in the Canadian Rockies.

The Icefields Parkway was specifically engineered to provide plenty of scenic viewpoints and information stations, knowing that you can't drive and stare ahead in awestruck wonder at the same time.

Started during the Great Depression as part of an unemployment relief project, this route between Lake Louise and Jasper is to now considered one of the world's great scenic highways.

ABOVE: Peacock-blue Pinto Lake is found east of the parkway and south of the Columbia Icefield. Beside it is Coleman Mountain, standing 3135 metres (10,285 ft).

A brief list of highlights includes Hector Lake, at the foot of the Waputik Range and icefield; Bow Lake, fed by water from the Bow Glacier, one of eight glaciers descending from the Waputik icefield; the Mistaya Valley, which passes a series of lakes before reaching Upper Waterfowl Lake with its stunning view of the Continental Divide; the Weeping Wall, its cliffs streaked with waterfalls fed by melting snow high up on Cirrus Mountain; Bridal Veil Falls and Panther Falls; Sunwapta Pass, the boundary between Banff and Jasper National Parks; the magnificent Columbia Icefield and Athabasca Glacier; Sunwapta Falls; Athabasca Valley, the longest and widest in the Rockies; Goats and Glaciers Viewpoint; and Athabasca Falls.

For a good time, turn around and drive back to Lake Louise. ∽

LEFT: This thin paved line parallels the Continental Divide.

70

SHEDIAC: LOBSTER CAPITOL
~ New Brunswick

You can enjoy locally caught lobster throughout Atlantic Canada, but only Shediac is willing to step up and proclaim itself "Lobster Capital of the World." A lobster features prominently on the town's logo, in its coat of arms and on the city flag.

This good-natured town of about 5,500 people is known for its lobster fishing, lobster processing plants, live lobster tanks and especially for its famous Lobster Festival, a five-day event held in early July.

The first Shediac Lobster Festival took place in 1949 and was a modest affair. Today's festival attracts some 50,000 visitors from all over the world, who come to feast on fresh, plentiful Shediac lobster and soak up Acadian and Maritime culture. There's a parade, a midway, and musical performances for the duration of the festival.

More than 50 types of fish and shellfish are caught in the region, but lobster reigns king in Shediac. Canada exports more than $1 billion worth of lobster annually, and New Brunswick operates by far the most lobster processing plants of any province. Here, a quartet of local lobster handlers presents a few of those billion-dollar crustaceans.

ABOVE: One of Shediac's most recognized landmarks is the giant lobster sculpture located at the western entrance to town. It is dedicated to sculptor Winston Bronnum, who finished work on the piece in 1990 and died the following year. The sculpture is 11 metres (35 ft) long, 5 metres (16 ft) high and weighs over 50 tons.

ABOVE: Traditional lobster buoys dry in the Shediac sun.

There's also a competitive, and ultimately hilarious, lobster-eating contest. Each night during the festival, three volunteers are chosen from the crowd to see how fast they can dissemble and consume three lobsters using only their bare hands.

Shediac is also the home of Parlee Beach Provincial Park, which is said to have the warmest saltwater north of Virginia, as well as beautiful white-sand beaches.

71 CHURCHILL'S POLAR BEARS
~ Manitoba

ABOVE: Why would the largest predator walking the Earth choose to live in one of the harshest environments? Ask this guy.

More than a thousand polar bears arrive at the tundra around Churchill each fall as they make their way to hunt for seals on Hudson Bay ice. This migration has occurred for centuries. The hungry bears don't exactly come *to* Churchill; it just happens that humans built a town on the spit of land that provides the most direct access to the seals. And if the bay isn't frozen when they get here, they tend to amble around in search of food to tide them over.

Polar bears can go long periods without food. Male bears have been known to go without a significant meal for three or four months when melting ice prevents them from hunting seals. Pregnant females are reportedly able to survive for as long as eight months.

BELOW: There's no road to Churchill. You must drive, fly or take a train to Winnipeg, then to Thompson, then continue by air or rail. There is a once-daily 9-seater flight from Winnipeg to Churchill. The train from Winnipeg to Churchill takes about 36 hours. Churchill is further north than most of us think it is.

ABOVE: Polar bears are typically solitary animals. Adult males can stand up to 3 metres (10 ft) tall on hind legs and weigh up to 680 kilograms (1,500 lbs), while females are smaller, weighing about 250 kilograms (550 lbs).

To survive these long fasts, polar bears must burn a thick layer of reserve fat. This layer also provides insulation against the extreme cold. The polar bear's small tail and ears, and double layers of fur also enable heat conservation. Its coat appears white because each hair is hollow and transparent, which serves to draw the sun's rays toward the bear's black skin.

You can make your way to Churchill and have your own private bear encounter, but it's ill advised. Go with a tour company. A number of reputable tour companies offer safe, informative excursions. Plan to go during October or November, when the bears are still gathering along the coast in anticipation of freeze-up. When the bay freezes, the bears travel far out onto the ice to hunt. If you arrive too late, just wait, the northern lights put on an amazing show in February.

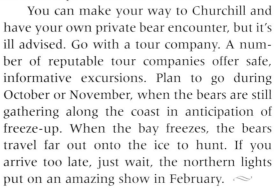

LEFT: The bears begin to arrive in late September or early October. November usually sees them in their greatest number, as the bears migrate toward Hudson Bay to await freeze-up. By mid-December the bay is usually iced over, and the bears have ventured further out to hunt.

72

GROS MORNE NATIONAL PARK
～ Newfoundland

LEFT: Gros Morne National Park's glacier-gouged fjords are part of the ancient beauty of Newfoundland's west coast landscape. The two-and-a-half-hour boat tours of Trout River Pond and Western Brook Pond are highly recommended. Looking up at billion-year-old cliffs from the deck of a boat deep inside a fjord is a simultaneously inspiring and humbling experience.

Gros Morne National Park's UNESCO World Heritage Site status comes not from its spectacular natural beauty — which it possesses in spades — but from its unique geology.

Almost six hundred million years ago, Europe and North America were a single supercontinent that was beginning to separate due to the shifting plates of the Earth's crust. Magma bubbled up from between the plates as the gap widened, and that cooled magma is now visible in the cliffs of Gros Morne's Western Brook Pond. To make a long geological story short, Gros Morne Park offers some of the world's best evidence of continental drift.

More recently, glacial action taking place over several ice ages has resulted in a remarkable combination of coastal lowlands, alpine plateaus, deep fjords, glacial valleys, sheer cliffs, spectacular waterfalls and some of the most pristine lakes found anywhere. The park's fjords are magnificent and alone are worth the long ferry ride from the mainland.

BELOW: When shrouded in mist, fog or covered in low clouds — as it often is — Gros Morne National Park takes on a mysterious appearance well suited to its ancient origins.

Gros Morne wildlife sightings are common, but it's interesting to keep in mind that animals now considered native to the island of Newfoundland made their way here over pack ice during the past 15,000 years. Newfoundland's isolation has resulted in a number of unique subspecies. Nine of its 14 native land mammals are distinct from their mainland relatives.

The Newfoundland black bear is generally larger than mainland species, and it has one of the longest hibernation periods of any bear in North America. The local species of Arctic hare is the world's southernmost and has the lowest reproductive rate of any hare or rabbit in the world, with one litter per year averaging only three young. Moose, however, seem made for the island. The first pair were brought here in 1878, with four more arriving in 1904. Today, they are found throughout Newfoundland, and the population density of moose in Gros Morne Park ranks among the highest in North America. ❧

ABOVE: A number of waterfalls spill down the high walls at Western Brook Pond, making this "freshwater fjord" seem somehow alive.

RIGHT: Some of the most ancient rock in the world can be seen in the cliffs of Western Brook Pond and Ten Mile Pond. The rocks of Gros Morne National Park and adjacent parts of western Newfoundland offer geologists vital information about the formation of ancient mountain ranges.

BELOW: Gros Morne is the second-highest mountain in Newfoundland. Arctic alpine tundra tops this 806-metre (2,644 ft) flat-topped peak, making it perfect habitat for more northerly species of plants and animals. The summit can be reached via a 16-kilometre (10 mi) trail.

73 YELLOWKNIFE ◆ CANADA'S DIAMOND CAPITAL
∽ Northwest Territories

Like many northern communities, Yellowknife owes its growth to gold. The precious metal was discovered up the Yellowknife River in 1933, and since that time, goldseekers have tried their luck, mining operations have come and gone, and the city's economy has struggled, thrived and struggled some more.

But in 1991, the discovery of diamonds 300 kilometres (190 mi) north of the city brought Yellowknife a new optimism and a fourth population boom. The Ekati diamond mine opened in 1998, and the Diavik mine in 2003. The following year, their combined production was estimated at $2.1 billion, putting Canada's diamond output third in the world by value. Operations by DeBeers are currently in development.

ABOVE: The city is located on the north shore of Great Slave Lake, on the west side of Yellowknife Bay near the outlet of the Yellowknife River. During the last week of March, the annual Caribou Carnival brings competitions and festivities to downtown's still-frozen Frame Lake.

BELOW: Yellowknife is a relatively young, modern city, with an ethnically mixed population. Five languages are spoken here in significant numbers: Chipewyan, Tli Cho, South and North Slavey, English and French.

ABOVE: The last of Yellowknife's gold mines closed in 2004. The city has turned its attention to diamonds, with 22 diamond-related operations listed in its business directory. Each diamond mined in the Northwest Territories comes with a certificate bearing the signature of the Premier and an assurance of quality and colour.

Yellowknife now calls itself "Diamond Capital of North America," and in 2005 the Northwest Territories Tourism Executive announced custom diamond tours for betrothed couples: "a once-in-a-lifetime journey through magnificent wilderness on a quest for the perfect diamond."

Billed as a "romantic learning adventure," the trip includes a private guided tour of the city, a charter plane flight to luxurious post-and-beam Blatchford Lake Lodge, a private dogsled excursion across frozen Great Slave Lake to view elusive indigenous wildlife, an "Arctic Expedition" with a personal chef, a catered show of the aurora borealis, a visit to Aurora College to learn more about diamonds, a consultation at the Gallery of the Midnight Sun regarding design and carat, a night of Dene hospitality, and finally a private visit to a Yellowknife diamond-cutting and -polishing facility to choose your stone, select your design and have your name laser-engraved for eternity on the girdle of the stone.

74

STANLEY PARK
~ British Columbia

Stanley Park is the largest city-owned park in Canada and, at 405 hectares (1,000 acres), one of the largest urban parks in North America. Surrounded by water on three sides and thick with old-growth forest, it was designated a National Historic Site because of the unique relationship between "its natural environmental and its cultural elements."

Much of the park remains forested. An estimated half million trees, some as tall as 76 metres (250 ft) and hundreds of years old, give Stanley Park its reputation as a wilderness oasis amid the bustle of one of Canada's busiest cities.

The park's famous seawall path offers pedestrians, runners, cyclists and skaters spectacular views, while wide trails lead to more serene spots in the wilder interior sections of the park and to Beaver Lake and Lost Lagoon.

Horse-drawn carriages come with professional guides to point out the park's many highlights, including Deadman's Island, Lions Gate Bridge, the Totem Poles, the *Girl in a Wet Suit* statue, the S.S. *Empress of Japan* figurehead, and the 3,000-species Rose Garden. The renowned Vancouver Aquarium is also located in the park. ~

ABOVE: Stanley Park's wilderness character comes from its forest. Walking trails lead through the park's dense rain-forest interior. A severe wind storm in December 2006 toppled or damaged thousands of trees.

RIGHT: The totem poles at Brockton Point are said to be the most visited tourist attraction in British Columbia. The initial four poles were from the Alert Bay region, some carved in the late 1880s. Later pieces were purchased from the Queen Charlotte Islands and Rivers Inlet. The badly weathered Skedans Mortuary Pole was replaced by a replica in 1962 and the remaining totems sent to museums for preservation. New poles were commissioned by or loaned to the Park Board between 1986 and 1992.

BELOW: Looking across Coal Harbour to the skyscrapers of downtown Vancouver from the east end of Stanley Park.

75

GRAND MANAN
~ New Brunswick

Grand Manan's only link to the mainland is a ferry that sails from Black's Harbour, New Brunswick. The ferry crossing takes 90 minutes, and as you watch the mainland disappear into the horizon, you begin to get a sense of this island's wild isolation.

This largest island in the Grand Manan archipelago is situated about 35 kilometres (22 mi) off the coast of New Brunswick, on the boundary between the Bay of Fundy and the Gulf of Maine. It stretches roughly 24 kilometres (15 mi) end to end and about 10 kilometres (6 mi) at its widest point. Its meadows teem with wildflowers; its houses and shops, painted lively colours, cling to their coves; and maritime history seems to hang in the salt air.

The western side of the island features steep cliffs, essentially an inaccessible wall against the sea, with the exception of tenacious Dark Harbour. Most of the island's population of around 3,000 live in the villages of North Head, Grand Harbour and Seal Cove.

Though the ferry ride lasts only 90 minutes, it feels like you've travelled decades, back to a quieter, simpler time, to a direct connection between people and the sea.

BELOW: Beneath barnacle-encrusted wharves, harbour pollock, sculpins, lumpfish, wreckfish and Atlantic wolf-fish, locally called "catfish," cruise for unsuspecting prey.

ABOVE: Quiet sunsets on Grand Manan have a restorative quality, but turbulent waters have claimed over 300 vessels around the island in the past two centuries.

BELOW: The largest island in the Bay of Fundy, Grand Manan is the home harbour for one of the world's great fisheries.

The surrounding ocean has supported a thriving fishery for generations of islanders, with scallops, herring, lobster and a great many other delicacies. These days, salmon aquaculture, seaweed-gathering and tourism round out the economy.

Grand Manan is a wonderful spot for whale-watching (humpback, minke, fin, pilot and right whale), as well as seals and white-sided dolphins. And though great white sharks are rare in the area, the world-record white, measuring 11.3 metres (37 ft) was captured off White Head in 1930. A bird sanctuary along the island's east shore has hosted over 400 species. ❧

76 DOGSLEDDING in QUEBEC
～ Quebec

Most parts of Canada that receive sufficient snowfall have dogsledding operations where you can mush or be mushed, but Quebec offers an extraordinary number of options and locations, from the Gatineau to the Laurentians, the Eastern Townships, up North, of course, and even 15 minutes outside Quebec City.

You can learn to drive your own four-dog team along groomed scenic trails or hang on tight as an expert driver guides a powerful nine-dog team through fresh powder. Not much beats the thrilling combination of crisp winter air and riding behind a determined dog team.

As well as being a centuries-old method of travel in much of Canada's Far North, dogsledding is also a link to our more recent past, to the fur traders, missionaries and gold prospectors who embraced Native ways to survive Canada's long winters.

Multi-day dogsledding trips have become a popular winter vacation alternative. It's now possible to end your dogsledding day with roughing-it-in-the-bush winter camping, a night in a charming bed-and-breakfast, or a stay at one of the province's finer lodges. And at least one Quebec operator offers sledders a night in an igloo. Excursions ranging from a few hours to as long as seven days are available in most regions. ～

ABOVE: Many consider the Siberian husky to be the best sled dog. Siberians' eyes can be brown, blue, amber or green, but they are one of the few dog breeds in which blue eyes are common.

LEFT: There's nothing quite like Nature's silence on a deep winter day, with just the panting of hardworking dogs and the sound of sled runners breaking trail through fresh snow. Watch for tracks made by rabbits, fox, deer and moose and other creatures.

RIGHT: Recommended attire for any dog-sledding adventure includes lightweight winter coat, fleece layering, snow pants, long underwear, gloves, snow boots, scarf, toque and a puppy.

77

NIAGARA FALLS & NIAGARA WINE COUNTRY
～ Ontario

When people speak of Niagara Falls, they invariably mean Horseshoe Falls, by far the largest of the three falls in the Niagara Falls gorge. The two smaller, but still impressive, falls are the American Falls and Bridal Veil Falls.

The falls formed with the receding of glaciers at the end of the most recent ice age. While not exceptionally high by world standards, Horseshoe Falls is wide, allowing an average 132.5 million litres (35 million gal) of water over its crest every minute, making it the most powerful waterfall in North America. (About half of this volume is currently diverted for hydro-electric power.)

Niagara Falls has long been considered North America's honeymoon capital. The phrase was used widely in advertising campaigns of the early 1900s. The first notable honeymooners were Theodosia Burr, daughter of U.S. Vice-President Aaron Burr, and husband Joseph Aliston in 1802. Napoleon Bonaparte's brother Jerome and wife Elizabeth Patterson are said to have honeymooned here shortly after.

Tourists of every nationality are provided with essential rain slickers before visiting the tunnels or stepping aboard the *Maid of the Mist*. It soon becomes one of two things they all have in common. The second is an awestruck smile that requires no translation.

ABOVE: The Canadian Horseshoe Falls span about 792 metres (2,600 ft) and tumble about 52 metres (170 ft) into the whirlpool below. In the 1800s numerous daredevils tempted fate by plunging over the falls in sealed containers or tightrope-walking above the gorge.

BELOW: The *Maid of the Mist* cruises have carried passengers into the whirlpools near the base of the falls since 1846. The boat begins its journey in calm waters near the Rainbow Bridge and slowly makes its way past the American Falls and Bridal Veil Falls before entering the dense spray of thundering Horseshoe Falls.

Niagara's wine route leads from one remarkable vineyard to another, passing through picturesque villages that offer some of Ontario's best theatre, dining, small museums and boutique galleries.

LEFT: Ontario wines now almost routinely win international awards and account for $500 million in retail sales.

BELOW: Located between 41 and 44 degrees North Latitude, the Niagara wine region is just south of France's Bordeaux region and parallel with northern California's best vineyards.

ABOVE: Ontario's Niagara vineyards are considered to be in a "cool" climate zone, which means that the harvested grapes will possess more concentrated flavours and balanced acidity.

BELOW: Wine country cycling routes are generally a mix of level and gently rolling terrain, mostly on bike paths and well-maintained country roads. Bike tours are available through several operators, with some providing options for those seeking a more challenging ride, and others providing van support for those desiring a lift, snack breaks or for transporting winery purchases.

Just beyond the falls' roar and the bustle of tourists is the peaceful, rolling countryside of Niagara's wine region. Nestled between the charming historic communities of Grimsby and Niagara-on-the-Lake, and protected by the high cliffs of the Niagara Escarpment, Niagara Peninsula vineyards quietly produce grapes for over 50 wineries. Decades of dedicated cultivation have led to wines that now receive international acclaim.

Often overlooked by visitors to Niagara Falls, the peninsula's wine region is an unusually sunny, temperate part of Canada, with northern California-like scenery. It's well worth a tour. ∾

78

GREAT NORTHERN ARTS FESTIVAL
~ Northwest Territories

For ten days each July, a handful of special guest artists from around the globe join over 100 artists from the Yukon, Northwest Territories and Nunavut to participate in the largest Visual Arts Festival in the North. Inuvik's popular arts festival features evening performances by Northern musicians, drummers and dancers, along with public workshops, artists' demonstrations, film screenings, the Great Northern Arts Festival fashion show, and legend sessions by local and visiting elders.

It has been said that this festival is noteworthy as much for its location as for its art and performances. For southern Canadians, this may well be true. A visit to the "True North" is an unforgettable experience

Represented are Inuit, Inuvialuit, Gwich'in, Tlingit, Dene, Metis and many of Canada's more southerly First Nations people, as well as non-Aboriginal artists and artisans. Participants often travel thousands of kilometres to show their work, meet other artists and learn new techniques.

First held in 1989, the festival has grown steadily every year since, with musicians and performers from as far away as Scotland's Orkney Islands and Mexico's Yucatan Peninsula. Recent visitors have come from all parts of Canada and the United States, as well as Japan, Germany, Denmark and Australia. In the spirit of inclusion, translators are on hand to translate Inuktitut and Inuvialuiktun to English. ~

LEFT: Workshops and demonstrations are held daily throughout the 10-day festival.

RIGHT: Patrons and participants can stroll among the displays and exhibits or even view artists at work. It is interesting to try to identify legends and motifs as they emerge from a stone, assemble from spare brushstrokes or take shape in the pattern of beads.

BELOW: The festival's opening and closing ceremonies involve traditional music and dance performances. In addition, an evening of drumming and dance features a variety of groups from the Mackenzie Delta area and is always a highlight.

79

ATHABASKA GLACIER
～ Alberta

LEFT: The Athabaska Glacier is one of six major glaciers that flow from Jasper National Park's Columbia Icefields, the largest sub-polar body of ice in North America.

Located between Banff and Jasper, the Athabasca Glacier is the most visited glacier on the North American continent. Spilling imperceptibly from Jasper National Park's massive Columbia Icefield, the glacier covers 6 square kilometres (2.5 sq mi) and stretches 6 kilometres (3.75 mi) down the valley. Its depth varies from 90 to 300 metres (270 to 1,000 ft).

Athabaska's ice is in constant motion, creeping downhill 125 metres (400 ft) per year, yet melting more than 1.5 kilometres (1 mi) over the past 125 years and losing half its volume.

The glacier is one of the six principal glacier "toes" that flow off of the Columbia Icefield, the remains of the thick ice mass that once mantled most of Western Canada's mountains (see Icefields Parkway page 204).

While it is tempting to wander off and attempt to climb partway up this ancient slab of ice, do not cross safety barriers. People have died from falling into the deep, hidden crevasses in this glacier. ～

BELOW: Brewster's Ice Age Adventure takes visitors on a 5-kilometre (3 mi) round-trip climb to the middle of the glacier in a specially designed Ice Explorer snow coach. At the halfway point, the coach stops and you can step out onto ice formed by snow that fell as long as 400 years ago.

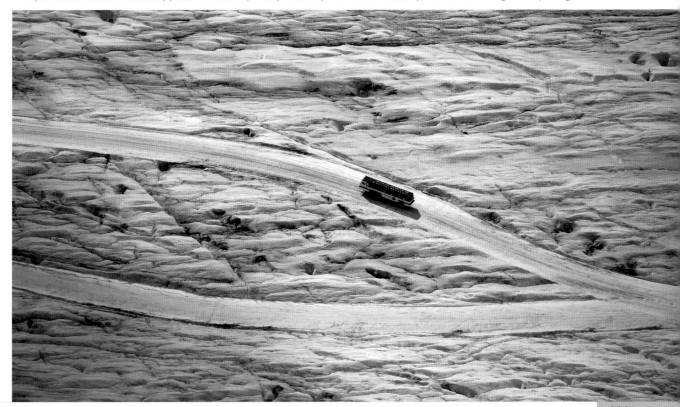

80

SIGNAL HILL NATIONAL HISTORIC SITE
~ Newfoundland

LEFT: Cabot Tower was built in 1897 in honour of the 400th anniversary of John Cabot's "Voyage of Discovery" and Queen Victoria's Diamond Jubilee. Today the tower contains exhibits and artifacts relating to Marconi's famous transatlantic radio reception at Signal Hill in 1901.

The first transatlantic wireless signal was received at Signal Hill by Guglielmo Marconi on December 12, 1901.

Signal Hill had long been used for observation and communication. Here, years before ship-to-shore radio, signalmen watched the ocean for ships headed into St. John's harbour, then raised coded flags from signal masts high atop the hill to convey information on approaching vessels to military and mercantile interests in St. John's.

Due to its strategic location, Signal Hill became the site of harbour defences from the eighteenth century through the Second World War. The last battle of the Seven Years War in North America was fought here in 1762.

BELOW: Looking across the entrance to St. John's harbour to Signal Hill, the historic site of the city's harbour defences from the eighteenth century to the Second World War.

Fortification began during the Napoleonic Wars. Queen's, Wallace's, Waldegrave, Duke of York's, Quidi Vidi Pass and Carronade batteries date from this period.

Three different hospitals were operated on the hill between 1870 and 1920. All of these were eventually destroyed by fire, but it was in the Diphtheria and Fever Hospital that Marconi received his famous transatlantic signal.

A Marconi Wireless Station operated on the second floor of Cabot Tower for many years. In 1920, one of the first wireless transatlantic transmissions of the human voice was made from the tower. Men at the station were able to talk with the steamship *Victoria* as it was steaming out of England. The station operated until around 1960.

On the St. John's side, a low wall suggests the wooden stockade wall and half-moon batteries that protected the summit from attack. Towards the narrows, a stone-walled viewing deck marks the area where the Duke of York's battery once stood. Other viewing bays on the seaward side of the summit provide breathtaking views of the ocean and surrounding coastline. ∽

Due to its strategic location, Signal Hill has a long history as an observation and communications point.

RIGHT: One of the site's most appealing attractions is an extensive walking trail, called the Lookout Trail, on the summit of Signal Hill. Along the trail, a number of interpretive panels explain important aspects of St. John's history, geography and climate.

BELOW: The steep streets and brightly painted wooden houses cascading down to St. John's inner harbour are a refreshing change from most cities' drab downtown residential areas.

81

BRACKENDALE
BALD EAGLES
~ British Columbia

LEFT: The bald eagle is the only eagle native to North America. They mate for life and can reach the age of 40. Breeding pairs remain together during nesting season to raise the young. Nesting activities begin in early April.

BELOW: The adult eagle's "bald" white head and tail feathers develop by its fourth or fifth year. Younger eagles have mottled brown and white plumage. The term "eagle-eyed" is well deserved, as an eagle can spot a fish in the water from more than a kilometre (.6 miles) away.

Brackendale Eagles Provincial Park lies in the Squamish River watershed of the Coast Mountains, about midway along the Sea to Sky Highway (#99). The new 550-hectare (1,360 acre) reserve protects important eagle habitat, keeping it off limits to logging, mining and other development.

The Squamish River Valley is one of the most significant areas in North America for wintering bald eagles. The watershed provides a perfect habitat, with a plentiful food supply due to significant runs of chum salmon in the Squamish, Cheakamus, and Mamquam rivers, and old-growth forests and large cottonwood trees for roosting. Two dozen or more eagles may roost in a single tree. It is often possible to see hundreds of eagles from the river dikes, either feeding along sandbars or roosting.

The eagles start to arrive in mid-November and remain until mid-February, with the largest concentration in late December to January. The local art gallery's annual January eagle count attracts visitors from around the world. A record count of 3,769 occurred in 1994. ~

82

CAPE ENRAGE
～ New Brunswick

C ape Enrage is the southern tip of Barn Marsh Island, about halfway between Riverside–Albert and Fundy National Park. The island is surrounded by jagged cliffs and separated from the mainland by a narrow tidal creek.

Cape Enrage's lighthouse, New Brunswick's oldest mainland lighthouse, claims bragging rights as the best place from which to watch the powerful forces of the Bay of Fundy. The Cape's 46-metre (150 ft) cliffs offer a panoramic view of the entire bay, from Apple River to Dorchester to Quaco.

Below the cliffs, Fossil Beach stretches more than 7 kilometres (4 mi), extending from the shores of Samurai Beach, around Lighthouse Point, across the ocean floor at low tide, and out to Brae Beach, an ancient Acadian dike. Visitors often spend hours walking this beach, hunting for fossils in the rock and shale.

Built in 1848 atop 46-metre (150 ft) cliffs, Cape Enrage lighthouse is still in use today.

ABOVE: *Frommer's Travel Guide* (2005) declared Cape Enrage's lighthouse view of the Bay of Fundy the "Best View in Canada."

The lighthouse was built atop the cliffs in 1848 and remains in use today, though without a keeper since the 1980s. The fully automated tower nonetheless sounds its foghorn and beams its beacon across the Bay of Fundy. By the early 1990s the keeper's house was abandoned and in serious disrepair. A group of local high-school students took on the task of restoring the historic dwelling.

LEFT: Adventure guides are available and can provide instruction on how to rappel down the Cape's magnificent cliffs (and how to climb back up again). Popular activities also include exploring the beach at low tide, sea-kayaking, guided caving trips, and fossil-hunting.

83

MOUNT ROYAL &
ST. JOSEPH'S ORATORY
～ Quebec

Mount Royal (Mont Royal) is the mountain for which the city of Montreal is named. Most Montrealers agree that a trip to the top of the mountain for a view of the city should be an essential part of any visitor's agenda.

The mountain stands some 200 metres (656 ft). Though not remarkably tall, it dominates the city's landscape, and its graduated terraces determined the city's settlement pattern for many decades.

Mount Royal Park was designed by renowned landscape architect Frederick Law Olmsted, who had already designed a number of large urban parks, including New York's famous Central Park. In 1872, with the city becoming congested due to rapid industrial and residential growth, land was expropriated on the mountain to create a park for all Montrealers.

This nighttime view shows many of Montreal's most recognizable modern buildings. The tallest structure at left is Place Ville-Marie, a distinctive 46-storey cruciform office tower that is, perhaps ironically, the hub of Montreal's underground city, the world's largest, with indoor access to over 1,600 shops, restaurants, cinemas and businesses, and several Metro stations. Place Ville-Marie's rotating rooftop beacon contains four spotlights that are visible for more than 50 kilometres (30 mi).

ABOVE: Tucked in among the downtown towers of commerce is Cathédrale Marie-Reine-du-Monde, the cathedral-basilica of Mary, Queen of the World. Construction began in 1875 on a basilica that was to be a scaled-down replica of St. Peter's in Rome. At the time of its consecration in 1894, it was the largest church in Quebec. The interior of the basilica is also modeled on St. Peter's. The cathedral was named a National Historic Site in 2006.

Olmsted conceived of the site as a natural environment park in the heart of the city. He sought to enhance the natural charms of the mountain. But he also wanted to encourage the mingling of all social classes. Olmsted's assigned a mere two-percent grade to the park's main access route (the future Chemin Olmsted) so that the one-horse carriages driven by families of lesser means could make it up the mountain.

Mount Royal Park has evolved and expanded, but the affection that Montrealers feel for this magnificent park has never changed.

LEFT: Mount Royal Park sees more than three million visitors a year. Many are tourists who have come to admire the views of the city from the park's lookouts and pathways, but the park is also one of the first places many former Montrealers must visit whenever they are in town.

The dome of St. Joseph's Oratory is second in size only to St. Paul's Basilica in Rome, and the church itself is said to be the largest in Canada. The basilica honours St. Joseph, whom faith healer Brother André credited for his miracles in healing the blind, deaf, sick and crippled. These miracles were authenticated by Pope John Paul II, and a wall of the basilica displays thousands of crutches belonging to those who once could not walk without them. More than two million pilgrims, worshippers and tourists visit the basilica each year.

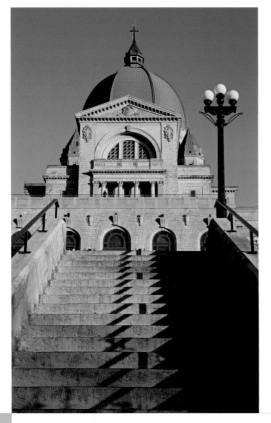

Saint Joseph's Oratory of Mount Royal is the highest, most visible building in Montreal. It began as a small chapel constructed in 1904 in honour of St. Joseph, husband of Mary, by a devout faith-healer named Brother André and his mostly blue-collar Congregation of the Holy Cross. Tens of thousands credited their miraculous healing to André's intervention with his patron, St. Joseph. Brother André's work was judged scandalous by many, but he became the most popular religious figure in Québec in the twentieth century.

St. Joseph's chapel soon became so crowded that a church with capacity for 1,000 was built in 1917. Work began on the 3,000-seat Oratory basilica in 1924. The Oratory's stated mission is to welcome pilgrims and accompany them on their spiritual journey, and the doors of the international sanctuary of St. Joseph's Oratory of Mount Royal are open to visitors of all walks of life.

St. Joseph's Oratory is only major urban shrine in Canada and remains the most important church in the world dedicated to St. Joseph.

84

GIMLI ICELANDIC FESTIVAL
∼ Manitoba

In Norse mythology, Gimli refers to the "home of the gods" or "high heaven" (the heaven above heaven). Though only about 2,000 people live in Gimli, it said to be home to the largest Icelandic population outside Iceland. A giant Viking statue greets visitors.

Gimli is located on the western shore of Lake Winnipeg, about 80 kilometres (50 mi) north of Winnipeg. When settlers arrived from Iceland in 1875, they dubbed their community New Iceland and set up an almost sovereign nation with its own government and laws. The following year, federal surveyors divided the republic of New Iceland into three townsites, one of which became Gimli, but New Iceland's independent government remained in place for another decade.

BELOW: During Islendingadagurinn, enthusiastic participants maintain a Viking encampment on Harbour Park Hill. The festival began in 1890 and is thought to be the second-oldest continuous ethnic festival in North America, after Montreal's annual Irish Festival.

ABOVE: Many know Gimli for its long, sandy beaches, its picturesque harbour, and its tastefully developed waterfront. Lake Winnipeg is a summer destination for many prairie-dwellers, and the Gimli Yacht Club holds a series of popular regattas. But few know that Manitoba has Canada's second-largest freshwater fishery and that half of those fish come from Lake Winnipeg.

Today, Icelandic and Norse Canadians celebrate their heritage each August long weekend with the Icelandic Festival of Manitoba, or Islendingadagurinn. Events include a parade through town, midway rides, a fine arts show, concerts, fireworks, sandcastle contest and running races.

More traditional Icelandic events include the recreation of a Viking encampment, the Islendingadunk (keyword "dunk") in Gimli Harbour, and the Fjallkona. The latter is the selection of a "Maid of the Mountain" (Fjallkona), who will wear formal Icelandic costume and sit on an elevated throne during the festival.

LEFT: As part of "The Path to Gimli," a horseback expedition retracing the route of Icelandic settlers in Canada, mail will be delivered by Icelandic post horse from Iceland to Canada, Pony Express style. Horses used in the expedition will be sold at a fundraising auction, with proceeds going to the Snorri Program, which provides grants to allow Icelandic Canadians to travel to Iceland and learn about their heritage.

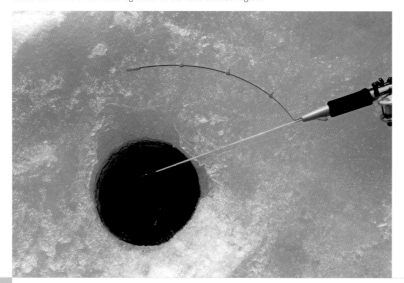

85

ICE-FISHING
on LAKE SIMCOE
~ Ontario

Lake Simcoe-area residents used to call their lake the Ice-Fishing Capital of North America, but a decade or so ago they hosted the World Championships of Ice-Fishing, and when international partici-pants said they'd never witnessed an event of comparable size, Lake Simcoe was promoted to Ice-Fishing Capital of the World.

The Canadian Ice-Fishing Championships are held here in late February, with over $50,000 in prizes. Additional trophies are presented for the Biggest Whitefish, Biggest Lake Trout, Top Scoring Male, Top Scoring Female, and Top Scoring Mixed Doubles Couple. Eight professionally trained officials score fish and make sure everyone follows CIFC rules.

On a good, cold winter weekend, there may be as many as 6,000 anglers on Lake Simcoe's ice surface. While that sounds like a big chunk of human-ity, it's worth noting that Simcoe is a big lake. Covering 743 square kilometres (287 sq mi) and fairly shallow, it is a perfect lake for ice-fishing.

The potential catch is diverse, with perch, walleye, pike, trout, herring, whitefish, bass and even muskellunge, though lake trout, walleye and white-fish are most common catches in winter. Bait choice depends on what you're after. Many ice-fishermen jig with grubs, cut bait, cheese balls or solid lures, but others swear by something called a Swedish Pimple.   ~

BELOW: Holes are generally made with powered augers or large chainsaws. When you rent a hut, the guy from the rental company is usually happy to cut a hole for you when he delivers the hut. There are over 30 hut rental agencies in the Lake Simcoe region.

ABOVE RIGHT: Ice and sun make a beauti-ful combination, but be sure to consult local outfitters regarding ice thickness and safety. Pressure ridges can build up in various spots on a lake and some areas may be thinner than others. Hut operators routinely scout the ice, check its thickness and estab-lish safe travel routes for foot traffic, snowmobiles, ATVs and full-sized vehicles.

RIGHT: Portable huts may be rented by the day or by the week. Some outfitters offer full icefishing vacations, with a heated fish-ing hut, pre-cut hole, a regularly replenished supply of bait, transportation to and from your hut, meal deliveries, and several nights in a local bed-and-breakfast.

86

MASSET POTLACH
~ British Columbia

ABOVE: The potlatch was a very important part of Haida social life. It was usually a lavish celebration of a wedding or birth. The ceremonies kept the old ways alive and taught the young people the history of their family. Often a clan's family lineage was recited, as well as the traditional rights of the family.

LEFT: A potlatch was often accompanied by the raising of a totem pole depicting events in the host's life, the life of his family or stories meant to be preserved.

The small village of Masset at the northern end of Graham Island is the largest in the Queen Charlotte Islands. A few minutes further up the coast is the Haida village of Old Masset, also known as Haida. Old Masset is the administrative seat of the Council of the Haida Nation and home to about 700 Haida, including some well-known carvers.

Potlatch ceremonies have been important events in the lives of Native people in the Pacific Northwest for centuries. These ritual feasts were traditionally held to celebrate a marriage or birth, the raising of a totem pole, or to honour the deceased. The host was, by necessity, a man of wealth and stature. He would invite hundreds of guests from his own clan and others, and these invitees would feast, perform spirit dances, sing and tell stories for as long as ten days. At the end of the potlatch, the host would give away many of his possessions as gifts to his guests. The celebration and such benevolent gestures proved the host's true worth. The more gifts he gave, the higher his status.

Of course, once the church and the federal government got wind of this, potlatches were banned straight away. And remained banned from 1884 until 1951. Apparently, giving away one's possessions showed a lack of respect for personal property.

Potlatches are legal once more and are still part of Haida culture, but they have become shorter, more modest celebrations — though no less colourful. It is a great honour to be invited to witness and participate in a potlatch, a lot of fun and a wonderful way to experience another culture, but don't expect to receive a handcarved Haida canoe from your host when you say goodbye. ~

LEFT: A family's carvers would contribute to potlatches by carving masks for the dancers or performing themselves. Dancers wore costumes and masks representing mythical ancestors and spirits. These masks, dances and songs were considered among the family's valuable possessions.

87

QUEBEC WINTER CARNIVAL & ICE HOTEL
∼ Quebec

LEFT: The Quebec Winter Carnival runs for 17 days at the end of January. The carnival's main venues see over a million visitors and participants every year.

Quebec City hosts the world's biggest winter carnival. Bonhomme, the big, friendly snowman in the toque and sash, oversees the proceedings.

Popular events include the annual canoe race on the St. Lawrence River between Quebec City and Lévis. In years when the river is iced over, teams pull their wooden canoes over the ice instead of paddling, but the show goes on. The Snow Bath sees a hundred or more hardy souls disrobe down to their bathing suits and execute three firm dives into the snow. There's dogsled racing, skating with Bonhomme, outdoor dance parties, night parades, fireworks, slide runs, concerts, snow sculpture competitions, horse-drawn sleigh rides, dogsled rides, the Ice Tower and ice-fishing. There's also a prestigious annual ball at Fairmont Le Château Frontenac.

BELOW: The carnival's official ambassador, Bonhomme Carnaval, looks on as bravely underdressed celebrants prepare for the bracing "snow baths," three quick plunges into the snow with brief goosebump intermissions.

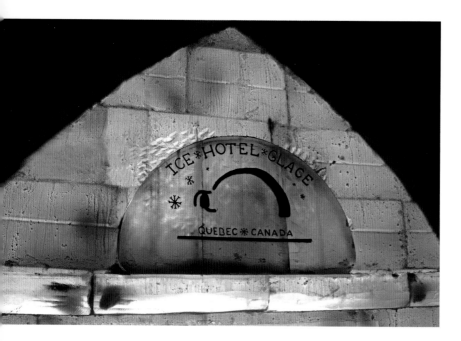

Just outside the city is the amazing Ice Hotel, inspired by the unique tourist attraction in the small Swedish village of Jukkasjärvi. The Ice Hotel opens for guests and visitors in early January and remains open until early April, or whenever the warm spring sun brings the melting establishment to a close for another year.

Constructed from 15,000 tons of snow and 500 tons of ice, the hotel has 5.4-metre (18 ft) ceilings and offers 36 rooms and suites, the N'Ice Club dancehall, the Ice Lounge, two art galleries, an Ice Chapel for custom weddings, and, most importantly, heated bathrooms. ～

RIGHT: Thirty-six rooms and suites provide accommodation for move than 88 people per night. "Imagine sleeping snugly in this luxurious structure crafted each winter from the purest of nature's materials: ice and snow," says the brochure. Maybe soak in the outdoor Ice Hotel hot tub before heading back to your ice suite and slipping into the sleeping bag.

88

BOUCTOUCHE DUNE
～ New Brunswick

LEFT: The Bouctouche dune reaches 12 kilometres (7.5 mi) into the bay at the mouth of the Bouctouche River. It is subtly reshaped by each major storm.

One of the last great dunes on the northeastern Atlantic coast, Bouctouche dune was created approximately 2,000 years ago by wind and currents from the north. In more recent years, J.D. Irving Ltd. developed the Irving Eco-Centre: La dune de Bouctouche to protect and preserve the dune and its unique ecosystem, and to educate visitors regarding its history and importance.

The dune's surface appears to be held in place by thousands of individual plants. Just below the surface, the interconnected horizontal root system forms one massive marram grass plant covering the entire dune. Without this net of vegetation, the dune would have disappeared centuries ago.

Instead, it serves as a habitat for a wide variety of native plants and animals, as well as a migratory stop for shorebirds and seabirds. The dune also protects the bay's calm inner harbour and its salt marshes.

RIGHT: A 2-kilometre (1.2-mi) boardwalk protects this extremely fragile environment from the steady march of tourists. Be careful not to disturb shorebird nests, including those of the endangered piping plover.

The salt-marsh coves provide a vital habitat for birds such as common terns, great blue herons and the endangered piping plover. Rare plants such as seaside pinweed and catfoot are also found on the sandbar.

The waters along the long stretch of sandy beach at the floor of the dune are surprisingly warm for most of the summer, and it is a pleasure to observe the activities of birds and mammals from the winding boardwalk. ～

89

WATERTON LAKES NATIONAL PARK
∽ Alberta

Alberta's Waterton National Park and Montana's Glacier National Park together comprise Waterton–Glacier International Peace Park, a UNESCO World Heritage Site.

Here, in the southwest corner of Alberta, Great Plains prairie plant species, northern Rocky Mountain plant species, and coastal species from the Pacific Northwest overlap to create many varied habitats in a single geographic location. These include grasslands, shrublands, wetlands, lakes; spruce, fir, pine and aspen forests; and alpine areas. More than half of all Alberta's plant species can be found in Waterton Park.

A small herd of bison is maintained at Waterton's Bison Paddock as a reminder of the large herds that once roamed this area. On Red Rock Parkway, an exhibit describes how jumps, corrals and other strategies were used by Native people to hunt bison in Blakiston Valley as much as 10,000 years ago.

ABOVE: The Prince of Wales Hotel sits on a bluff overlooking Upper Waterton Lake. It was built by the Great Northern Railway and opened in 1927. Its name is said to have been an attempt to entice the Prince of Wales (later King Edward VIII) to stay at the hotel during his 1927 Canadian tour. The Prince did not stay at the Prince of Wales, but the hotel is fit for royalty, with its alpine chalet atmosphere and spectacular view of the Rockies.

The park's wide variety of vegetation provides homes, and in some cases food, for more than 60 species of mammals, over 250 species of birds, 24 species of fish, and 10 species of reptiles and amphibians. Large predators such as cougars, grizzly bears and American black bears roam higher elevations, while the grasslands support elk, mule deer and white-tailed deer in their winter range. A number of rare or unusual animals are also found here, including trumpeter swans, Vaux's swifts and vagrant shrews.

The Waterton Lakes chain (Upper, Middle and Lower Waterton lakes and the Maskinonge) makes up almost two thirds of the total water surface area in the park. The international boundary separating Canada and the U.S. runs in an invisible line across Upper Waterton Lake about halfway down its length, making the lake the right symbol for UNESCO-honoured Waterton–Glacier International Peace Park. ∽

LEFT: Moose, elk, mule and white-tailed deer, bison, bighorn sheep and mountain goats can be seen throughout the park.

90

TEA at the EMPRESS
~ British Columbia

Tea at the Empress has been a tradition since this regal hotel opened in 1908. The hotel is famous far and wide for its elegant Afternoon Tea, prepared and served in true British tradition, accompanied by berries and Chantilly cream, scones, crumpets, preserves, sandwiches, pastries and tarts, all served with silver service in the main lobby. Over 75,000 visitors each year take part in this posh ritual.

The Fairmont Empress is considered to be the most photographed attraction on Vancouver Island, and high tea is a highlight of any visit to Victoria. Rising above the city's Inner Harbour, the 460-room hotel was designed in the Edwardian style by architect Francis Rattenbury a century ago.

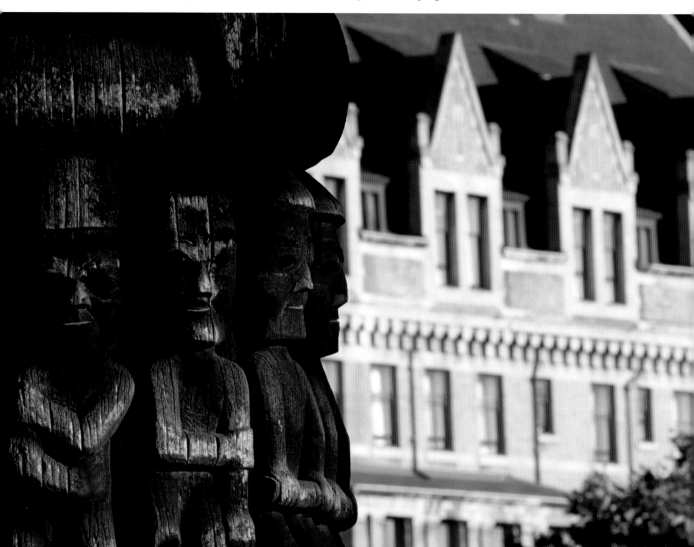

Afternoon Tea is
served with silver service
in the main lobby.

LEFT: In 1965 it looked as though the fading Empress might be torn down to make room for a modern high-rise hotel, but on June 10, 1966, it was announced that the hotel would receive a $4-million renovation. This became known as "Operation Teacup."

The hotel has entertained such celebrities as Rita Hayworth, Jack Benny, Pat O'Brien, Douglas Fairbanks, Shirley Temple, Katherine Hepburn, Bob Hope, Bing Crosby, Tallulah Bankhead, Roger Moore, Barbara Streisand and Harrison Ford. Kings and queens have also experienced the hotel's many charms. There are those who still fondly recall the night in 1919 when Edward, Prince of Wales, waltzed until dawn in the Crystal Ballroom.

A $45-million "Royal Restoration" recently returned the grand dame of western hotels to her original grandeur.

LEFT: Comfortably situated amid the distinctive scenery and iconography of the Canadian West Coast, the Empress has enchanted guests and visitors since 1908. Today's Fairmont Empress retains its original charm and grandeur while offering all the trappings of a modern luxury hotel.

RIGHT: When workers raised The Empress sign above the front entrance following elaborate renovations, one gentleman of character was heard to say, "Anyone who doesn't know this is The Empress shouldn't be staying here."

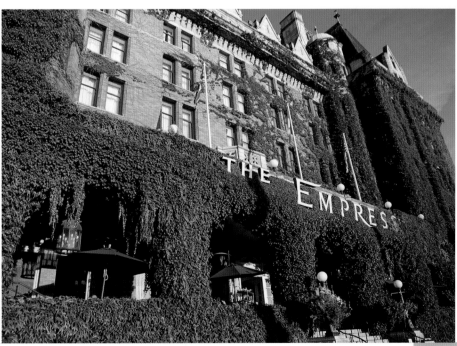

KLUANE NATIONAL PARK
~ Yukon Territories

Kluane National Park and Reserve covers an area of 21,980 square kilometres (8486 sq mi). It is a land of high mountains, vast icefields and alpine valleys. Kluane is also home to Canada's highest peak, Mount Logan.

The park's chain of mountains averages 2500 metres (8,000 ft) in height. To the west lie the rugged Icefield Ranges, whose peaks double that height, vaulting into the 5000-metre (16,000 ft) range.

BELOW: Kluane National Park and Reserve is dominated by mountains and ice. The St. Elias Mountains, Canada's highest and most massive range, are actually two ranges separated by a narrow trough known as the Duke Depression.

The world's largest non-polar icefields have developed from the massive quantities of snow that accumulate over the St. Elias Mountains. Glacial movements often initiate dramatic transitions. Around 1850, Lake Alsek is said to have drained in two days after its ice dam broke, producing a flow rate comparable to that of the Amazon River. The flooding associated with such advances and retreats of Naludi (Lowell Glacier) is chronicled in many legends and stories by the Southern Tutchone people.

BELOW and LOWER RIGHT: Dall's sheep are Kluane's most abundant mammal and can often be seen grazing on appropriately named Sheep Mountain. The park has the world's greatest concentration of Dall's sheep.

ABOVE: These are not roads. This image of Kaskawulsh Glacier, with Mt. Kaskawulsh in the centre, shows how glaciers are really rivers of ice. The flow of the glacier has been divided, creating a medial moraine in the process.

With its combination of Pacific and Arctic air, Kluane National Park and Reserve provides a perfect habitat for many species of wildlife, particularly Dall's sheep, but also mountain goats, caribou, North America's largest subspecies of moose, grizzly bears, black bears, a transient population of wolves, and smaller mammals such as wolverines, muskrats, mink, marmots, red fox, lynx, otter, coyotes, beavers, snowshoe hares and Arctic ground squirrels.

92

CANADIAN MINT
⌇ Manitoba

This is where your money comes from. The Royal Canadian Mint in Winnipeg produces all of Canada's circulation coins, from the 1-cent coin to the bi-metallic $2 coin. The Mint also produces circulation currency for other nations. Over the last 20 years, the Mint has produced over 14 billion coins for other countries, with high-speed coining presses that can each strike as many as 750 coins a minute.

The Winnipeg plant features state-of-the-art computer and robotic systems, environmentally sound plating processes, automated units capable of inspecting 180,000 blanks per hour, and over 40 coining presses with potential production of 15 million plated coins per day. The Mint also designs and manufactures collector coins, gold and silver bullion coins, customized medals, tokens and trade dollars, watches, jewellery and gifts.

Gold Maple Leaf coins set the standard for world bullion coins with .9999 fine gold purity. It remains one of the world's finest investment coins.

Be sure to visit the provincial legislature building while in Winnipeg. The building is famous for its gold-covered bronze statue, "Golden Boy," at the top of its cupola. In the main entrance is the Grand Staircase, with steps of brown-veined Carrara marble. On either side of the steps are life-size solid-bronze bison. The bison were cast at the Roman Bronze Works in New York City. Each bison weighs 2.5 tons. To install the bison without damaging the marble floors, the main entrance was flooded and left to freeze. The bison were then placed on enormous slabs of ice cut from the Assiniboine River and slid safely into the building.

ABOVE: For Winnipeg's Royal Canadian Mint, architect Etienne Gaboury designed a striking triangular form that would soar above the prairie. Glazed walls give the tower the appearance of a crystalline prism that also suggests the facility is a modern, high-security building. Its walls are massive and all windows are either very high or over water.

Who would believe that the platypus-faced Australian 20-cent coin was made in Canada? If it was minted in 1981, it was among 50 million produced in the Winnipeg plant. To date, the Royal Canadian Mint has produced coins for over 74 countries, including Cuban centavos, Yemen fils, Colombian pesos, Icelandic kroner, rupiah for Indonesia, baht for Thailand, and a thousand-dollar coin for Hong Kong. The Winnipeg production branch of the Royal Canadian Mint is one of the largest and most respected minting operations in the world. ◁

LEFT: Canadian coin designs have won 15 major international awards since 1985.

93

ENTRY ISLAND
~ Quebec

Entry Island is the English one. Located 10 kilometres (6 mi) to the east of Amherst Island in the Magdalens, Entry Island is accessible only by boat. Entry can be identified by its steep cliffs, the highest one rising 170 metres (550 ft) above the water. The highest point of land in the Magdalen archipelago is on Entry Island.

The English population of the Magdalens was once distributed among all the islands, in primarily Francophone communities such as Havre-Aubert, Cap-aux-Meules, Havre-aux-Maisons and Etang-du-Nord, but the English population declined as residents left the islands to look for work. Soon Anglophones made up only five percent of the islands' population, mainly concentrated in the municipalities of Grosse Ile and Entry Island. Less than 130 residents of Scottish and English descent now inhabit "the English island."

The island has two stores, a restaurant, church, school, museum, post office, and a bed-and-breakfast that operates during the tourist season.

BELOW: English communities exist on three of the Magdalen Islands, but Entry Island is the only community not connected to the others by sand dunes or highway. Entry Island is accessible only by sea.

ABOVE: One recent visitor referred to the island's pastoral splendour as *"Brigadoon-like fields of grasses and wildflowers."* The hills offer magnificent views of the almost treeless, rolling landscape. There are no shortages of perfect picnic spots.

A regular local ferry service operates from May until the end of December. Entry Island is a beautiful place to spend a few leisurely days in relative isolation, looking out to sea from its high hillsides, strolling the footpaths along the coast, visiting the local museum, enjoying picnics and meals at La Grave, and listening to island musicians at Theatre au Vieux Treuil. ∽

94

DELLA FALLS
~ British Columbia

Vancouver Island's Della Falls is the highest waterfall in Canada. It tumbles 440 metres (1,444 ft) in three cascades from Della Lake. What Della Falls lacks in thunderous volume, it makes up for in height and location.

There are basically two choices for getting to the falls: you can hire a helicopter or you can make your way to Port Alberni, cross Great Central Lake by boat (about 20 km/12 mi) to the Strathcona Provincial Park dock, and follow the rocky climbing trail for about eight hours to reach the base of the falls. Of course, we recommend the latter. It's not a bad idea to camp after crossing Great Central Lake and take on the hike the next day.

Part of the hike follows the bed of an old logging railway, which in turn follows Drinkwater Creek through magnificent forests past a series of warm-up-for-Della waterfalls. Providing background scenery are the peaks of Big Interior Mountain, Mount Septimus and Nine Peaks, each over 1800 metres (5,905 ft). Drinkwater Creek is named for prospector and trapper Joe Drinkwater, who discovered Della Falls in 1899. (Della was his wife.) Drinkwater started the Ark Resort, "Gateway to Della Falls," which is still in operation. ~

ABOVE: Located in Strathcona Provincial Park, Della Falls has a vertical drop of 440 metres (1,444 feet), making it almost seven times higher than Niagara's famous Horseshoe Falls.

LEFT: Created in 1911, Strathcona Provincial Park is the oldest provincial park in British Columbia. It is a rugged wilderness area at its higher elevations, with glaciers, snowfields and mountains in excess of 1800 metres (5,905 ft).

RIGHT: Della Lake is the basin that feeds Della Falls. Prospector Joe Drinkwater discovered Canada's highest falls in 1899 and named the falls, and the lake above them, for his wife, Della.

95

Lucy Maud Montgomery's
CAVENDISH NATIONAL HISTORIC SITE
∽ Prince Edward Island

The land of Anne of Green Gables is a point of pilgrimage for Lucy Maud Montgomery fans worldwide. Montgomery is said to have found inspiration for her first novel in a newspaper article about a couple mistakenly sent an orphan girl instead of a boy, but much of her 1908 classic and her subsequent books are based on her own childhood experiences in rural Prince Edward Island.

Soon after *Anne of Green Gables* was published, enamored readers began descending on Cavendish in search of Green Gables and other settings and characters of Avonlea. The book has since been translated into 17 languages, and Anne-related tourism is now an important part of PEI's economy. Montgomery's novels are particularly popular in Japan, attracting some 6,000 Japanese visitors to Green Gables each year.

Shortly after her death in 1942, Montgomery was recognized by the Historic Sites and Monuments Board of Canada as a person of national historic significance, and a monument and plaque were erected at Green Gables in 1948. The site has recently seen the reconstruction of a period barn, granary and woodshed. The house has been restored to reflect the late 1800s, the time period depicted in *Anne of Green Gables*. Of Montgomery's 20 novels, 19 are set in Prince Edward Island.

PEI's rich red soil is a part of the island's setting *and* character. The land's distinct coloration is due to its high iron-oxide content. The island was formed from a sedimentary bedrock of soft, red sandstone.

BELOW: In the nineteenth century, farm families produced most of what they needed to survive. Any surplus could be used to trade for other goods or services. According to census figures, the Montgomerys' cousins the Macneills produced 360 pounds of cheese and 260 pounds of butter in 1861.

ABOVE: Part of the Lucy Maud Montgomery National Historic Site, the Green Gables property is famous around the world as the inspiration for the setting in the *Anne of Green Gables* series. The farm was the home of David and Margaret Macneill, cousins of Montgomery's grandfather. The Macneills' niece, Mrytle, married Ernest Webb, and they were the last of the family to operate the farm. Montgomery often stayed with the Webbs on her return visits to the island.

Also on your "I Love Anne" agenda should be the Lucy Maud Montgomery Heritage Museum, Anne of Green Gables Heritage Museum, Avonlea Village, Green Gables Post Office, Lucy Maud's Cavendish Homestead, and Lower Bedeque Schoolhouse, where Montgomery taught. A Lucy Maud Montgomery Festival occurs each August, as well as Parks Canada's popular Halloween in the Haunted Wood and A Green Gables Christmas. ✑

96

KITIKMEOT & BEECHEY ISLAND HISTORIC SITE

◡ Nunavut

Kitikmeot, or Qitirmiut in Inuktitut, is one of three administrative regions within Nunavut. It includes southern and eastern parts of Victoria Island, the nearby mainland as far as the Boothia Peninsula, as well as King William Island and the southern part of Prince of Wales Island.

Though the land is ancient and the region's cultural history goes back thousands of years, this region's importance in European history dates to the 1570s, when various explorers set out to discover a commercial sea route north and west around mainland North America. This hypothetical route known as the Northwest Passage brought numerous expeditions to these waters over the next 300 years, and many explorers' names live in Anglicized place names, but it wasn't until 1906 that anyone successfully navigated through the Arctic archipelago from Atlantic to Pacific.

A community igloo near Gjoa Haven. An experienced builder can construct an igloo in 20 to 30 minutes. Blocks of snow are cut from snowbanks using a snow knife and are arranged in a spiral pattern (not row upon row), working toward the top of the dome. The best snow comes from a snowbank formed by a single snowstorm.

BELOW: Inside a traditional igloo at Gjoa Haven. The Inuktitut name for the community is Uqsuqtuuq, which means "lots of fat." Blubber-bearing sea mammals live in abundance in the surrounding waters.

ABOVE: Before Roald Admundsen's first successful navigation through these waters, explorers had spent centuries searching for the seemingly mythical Northwest Passage from the Atlantic to the Pacific. In the words of Nunavut Tourism: "This *is* the Northwest Passage. This *is* the Arctic."

The man who accomplished this feat was Norwegian Roald Amundsen, who is said to have departed on his voyage three years earlier, in a hurry to escape his creditors. His vessel was a 47-ton herring boat called *Gjoa*.

In October of 1903, seeing that the Arctic straits were beginning to ice up, Admundsen entered a natural harbour on the south coast of King William Island. Admundsen called it "the finest little harbour in the world," and there he and *Gjoa* remained for the next two years. He learned all he could from the Netsilik Inuit, and adopted their lifestyle and dress. This harbour's English name became Gjoa Haven.

ABOVE: Wind-weathered markers announce the final desolate port of call for four Victorian sailors. Inscriptions tell the tale of a Royal Marine, an able seaman and a stoker who died with the Franklin expedition in 1846; the fourth man, a sailor, met his end while on a search mission to find and rescue Franklin.

RIGHT: German adventurer Arved Fuchs attempted to reenact Admundsen's 1903–06 journey, but his ship, the *Dagmar Aaen*, was forced to overwinter in Cambridge Bay while he returned to Germany to raise additional funds.

Many earlier expeditions failed to find such a harbour or such hospitality. In 1845, Sir John Franklin chose the protected harbor of Beechey Island for his first winter encampment. When British and American search vessels anchored nearby in 1851, they discovered the graves of three of Franklin's crew: Petty Officer John Torrington, Royal Marine Private William Braine, and Able Seaman John Hartnell. However, there was nothing to indicate where Franklin planned to sail. The fate of his remaining crew remained a mystery for another 140 years, until the bodies from the ill-fated Franklin expedition were found at Gjoa Haven on King William Island.

RIGHT: The grave marker for John Hartnell of H.M.S. *Erebus* is a replica. The original resides in the Prince of Wales Heritage Centre in Yellowknife.

97

BANFF SPRINGS HOTEL
~ Alberta

LEFT: The CPR's William Cornelius Van Horne saw the tourism potential of the Canadian West. He envisioned a collection of luxurious CPR-owned resort hotels along the company's line through the Rocky and Selkirk Mountains. "Since we can't export the scenery," said Van Horne, "we'll have to import the tourists."

Surrounded by the spectacular scenery of Old Squaw Mountain, Mt. Norquay, Cascade Mountain and Mt. Rundle, Banff is the Canadian Rockies' premier tourist destination. In keeping with its status, it also boasts the largest number of hotels, inns and bed & breakfasts. But none compare to the majestic Banff Springs Hotel.

The hotel is built in the design of a Scottish baronial castle. Its main view looks across the Bow Valley to distinctive Mt. Rundle, a 330-million-year-old seabed thrust upward at a striking angle. Nearby are Banff's thermal hot springs and Bow Falls, which was a setting in the 1953 Marilyn Monroe film *The River of No Return*.

Canadian Pacific Railway general manager William Cornelius Van Horne hired leading New York architect Bruce Price to make his vision of a chateau-style luxury hotel at the convergence of the Bow and Spray rivers a reality. Banff Springs Hotel opened on June 1, 1888.

Famous guests have included King George VI and Queen Elizabeth. And the story goes that Benny Goodman is responsible for Banff obtaining a landing strip. Goodman would only stay at the hotel if there were proper place to land his personal plane.

BELOW: Styled after a Scottish baronial castle, the Fairmont Banff Springs offers stunning vistas, championship golf courses, unparalleled skiing, exquisite cuisine and a world-class European-style spa.

Few hotels have been able to approximate the Fairmont Banff Springs Hotel's combination of elegant hospitality and breathtaking scenery. It has been a world-recognized landmark of Rocky Mountain grandeur for more than a century. ~

REVERSING FALLS
～ New Brunswick

Twice a day, at low tide, the 724-kilometre (450 mi) St. John River empties itself into the Bay of Fundy through a narrow, rocky gorge. Near Saint John's Fallsview Park, an underwater ledge causes a series of rapids and whirlpools. The rising tide slows the river current to a stop, and during this 20-minute "slack tide," boats are able to navigate the falls.

Once the tide becomes higher than the river, the reversal of the current occurs and continues until high tide. The river's natural south-facing mouth receives the ocean's tides like a funnel. The tide drops slowly but continues to flow inland until it reaches river level again. But after 20 minutes of "high slack," the river resumes its natural flow and the tide drops away to low tide, once more revealing the rapids and whirlpools. The effect of this reversal is felt upstream as far as Fredericton, more than 128 kilometres (80 mi) inland.

Sight-seeing tours and jet-boat thrill rides can be booked at Fallsview Park in Saint John. For a more extreme experience, you can be harnessed into The Bubble, which allows its rider to "bounce through rapids, spin in whirlpools and flip through the whitecaps of the mighty Reversing Falls."

When the tide is low, the St. John River empties into the bay. Between Fallsview Park and the pulp mill, the river's full flow rushes through a narrow gorge, where an underwater ledge causes the water to tumble downward into a deep pool under the bridge, creating a series of rapids and whirlpools.

Bay of Fundy tides are
the result of surging tides
in the Indian Ocean
as they round the
Cape of Good Hope.

To really appreciate the Reversing Falls, try to view them at least twice, near low tide and high tide. Fallsview Park is a great place from which to view the falls. The park also has a Reversing Falls Information Centre, with a short film explaining the phenomenon.

Of course, nothing beats the full-spray encounter that a Reversing Falls jet-boat ride provides. You really can't expect to fully comprehend all this tidal hydro-babble until you've been "at one" with it. ⌒

99 CRUISING the ST. LAWRENCE
~ Quebec

On St. Lawrence's Day in 1535, explorer Jacques Cartier gave that saint's name to a small bay near the great river's mouth. By 1600, St. Lawrence was in common use as the name for the entire river.

For successive waves of explorers, traders and settlers, the St. Lawrence River was the quickest route to North America's interior, with its vast lands and rich cache of resources. It was, and remains, the continent's great inland waterway, reaching deep between the Laurentians and the Appalachians to the Great Lakes.

The province of Quebec is underscored by the St. Lawrence River, and since the sixteenth century, the river has been both home and livelihood for the generations who settled its shores and learned its ways.

The Laurentian Mountains, north of the river, are among the world's oldest mountain ranges.

More than 20 tour companies offer Quebec-based St. Lawrence River cruises lasting from a couple of hours to a couple of weeks, with side trips or lay-overs available for almost any shoreline city, historic village or island destination you might wish to visit.

ABOVE: A sunset cruise through the islands and islets of Bic National Park near Rimouski. The park abounds with capes, bays, coves, islands and mountains, as well as thousands of seabirds and noisy colonies of sun-basking harp seals.

BELOW: This boat is headed to the Magdalen Islands. Cruises to the Magdalens often include sightseeing trips along the river's south shore and select Gaspé Peninsula locations, as well. The seaview trails of Forillon National Park are a great place to sight humpback whales.

Scenic highways run along both shores of the St. Lawrence, but many of the most stunning vistas in Quebec are best viewed from the deck of a ship plying these historic waters. The waterway flows over 1100 kilometres (685 mi) along Quebec shorelines, and informative cruises are a wonderful way to visit such locations as the Saguenay River Fjord, the sensational cliffs above the Malbaie River, the islands of the Mignan Archipelago, and the picturesque villages of Harrington Harbour and Blanc–Sablon.

Boat operators in Montreal and Quebec City offer port tours, dinner cruises or romantic evening cruises that feature unrivalled views of these cities. The more open waters of the estuary and gulf are home to over a dozen whale species, including belugas and blue whales.

Whether you are interested in marine life, natural wonders, centuries-old fishing villages, cosmopolitan Quebec cities or quiet islands in the sea, there is a cruise boat waiting to welcome you aboard. ～

100

SALMON FISHING in the QUEEN CHARLOTTE ISLANDS
~ British Columbia

LEFT: Anglers from around the world come to the Queen Charlotte Islands for the exceptional salmon fishing. The islands are the first land in the path of Pacific chinook, coho and chum salmon as they migrate south from their Arctic feeding grounds to their spawning grounds in the Pacific Northwest.

The Queen Charlotte Islands are Mecca to the world's salmon fishermen. Some anglers may come in search of tuna, halibut, herring or trout, but salmon reigns king in these waters — at least during their annual migrations.

This spectacular island archipelago is the first land to interrupt the migratory path of Pacific chinook, coho and chum salmon as they journey south to their spawning grounds in the Pacific Northwest. The islands are the best location from which to intercept millions of well-fed salmon en route from their Alaska feeding grounds.

BELOW: The Queen Charlottes are known to the Haida as Gwaii Haanas, meaning "Place of Wonder." In a recent issue, *National Geographic Traveler* magazine voted Gwaii Haanas National Park Reserve and Haida Heritage Site the #1 National Park in North America.

ABOVE: There's nothing quite like battling a 23-kilogram (50 lb) giant chinook. Chinooks are also called king salmon because of their large size and food value. Chinooks over 14 kilograms (30 lb) are called Tyees.

ABOVE: Fly-in lodges combine world-class fishing with five-star cuisine and a full range of hotel-like services.

LEFT: The seas around Gwaii Haanas are home to salmon, herring, halibut, tuna, lingcod, rockfish, mussels, clams, crabs, octopi, and dozens of other desirable catch species.

The Queen Charlottes are among the best places to catch a "king" — a massive chrome-coloured chinook salmon.

All-inclusive fishing holidays can be booked directly or through most tour companies. The West Coast Fishing Club offers perhaps the most elegant packages, with multiple locations and lodges, an extensive fleet of boats, top guides, and a full staff that includes several professional chefs, but more modest options are available. The season is roughly from June to September, but check local information when booking.

A typical day's salmon fishing may include ten hours on the water, but experienced guides also find time for whale-watching opportunities and sidetrips to ancient Haida ruins.

While in Masset, try digging for razor clams on Naikoon Provincial Park's North Beach at low tide. Small, round depressions in the sand indicate likely locations. If the sand moves when touched, you've found a clam. Good luck, though; you'll be surprised how fast a limbless little mullusk can dig. ⌒

Noel Hudson's
ACKNOWLEDGMENTS

I have been fortunate over the years to work with and befriend several knowledge-able and talented Canadian adventurers, people who, given a canoe and a waterway, are happy to disappear into remote Canadian landscapes for weeks or months at a time. My sincerest gratitude to James Raffan, Kevin Callan, Gary and Joanie McGuffin, and Donald Standfield for allowing us to use some outstanding photographs from their travels.

For their kind assistance with images for some of the prairie locations, I would like to thank Becky Poley-Schutz, Belva Schlosser and Daryl Demoskoff at Tourism Saskatchewan, and Erin Larson, Louise Beauchamp and Laureen Dirksen at Alberta Tourism and Alberta Economic Development.

Thanks to my Montreal Jazz Festival accompanist Steve Bolton for another inspir-ing musical excursion; to my long-time BC pals Calvin Wharton and Julian Ross for keeping me connected to that province; to Mary Ann McLean and Ian Macdonald for introducing me to Alberta hoodoos and prairie sedges; to Michael Bedford for convinc-ing me to spend a year in Quebec; to Liza Wendt and Kevin Jeffrey in PEI for the Norseboat bunkhouse; and to the Mahoneys of Holyrood, Newfoundland, for their unri-valled hospitality (and for the "bottled rabbit" to go).

Thanks to Kathy Fraser and John Denison, my long-time friends and colleagues at Boston Mills Press, for their valuable suggestions and support; and to the Firefly Books crew, especially Kim Sullivan in Production.

Thanks to George Fischer for another book of stellar photography. George travelled Canada up, down and sideways to get these shots, often in uncooperative weather and fighting a flight deadline, yet he managed to capture magic at every stop.

And big thanks to my best friend, wife and book designer, Gill Stead, for another great design, an unboring life, and three adventurous offspring, Marin, Walker and Tess, who are always ready to take a trip — even a car trip through six provinces.

George Fischer's
ACKNOWLEDGMENTS

This book would not have been possible to produce without the generous support of our Canadian partners and sponsors. In particular I would like to express my gratefulness to Randy Brooks of the Nova Scotia Dept. of Tourism, Culture and Heritage; Mike Taylor and Lori Grant of Fairmont Hotels and Resorts; Mattias Peemoeller of the Fairmont Empress Hotel; Trista Zamany, Lesley Heal, Marianna Matejkova, Cathy Leblanc of the Fairmont Empress Hotel for the Tea Party; Marie-France Dubois of the Fairmont Chateau Lake Louise; Linda Ungar and Judith Venaas of Northwest Territories Tourism; Neil Hartling of Nahanni River Adventures; Ted Grant of Simpson Air, Fort Simpson; James and Maureen Pokiak of Ookpik Tours; Gillian Earle of Avis Canada; Captain John Pynn and Thomas Eddison of Adventure Boat Tours, L'Anse aux Meadows; Nancy Dery of Rocky Mountaineer Vacations; Debra Ryan of Air North, Yukon's Airline; Debbie Martell of the Cape Breton Highands Project; Gary DeYoung of 1000 Islands Tourism Council; Brian Grange of the Westcoast Fishing Club; Andrew Merilees of Northwest Recreation Services; Andrew Jones of Kingfisher Wilderness Adventures; Joel Lagasse, Kingfisher Wilderness Adventures; Irene Knight of CN Tower/La Tour CN; Maid of the Mist, Niagara Falls; Catharine Barker of National Graphics; Luba Plotnikoff of Oceanside Tourism Association; Ted Hedderson of Burnt Cape Cabins; Betsy Foster of Tourism Niagara; Laird Robertson Consulting; Fiona McIntosh of Niagara Cellars Inc./Diamond Estates; Nahman Korem of Crown Jewel Resort, Baddeck; Jim Kemshead of Yukon Tourism; Lana Kingston of Tourism Vancouver Island; Heidi Wesling, Tourism Vancouver Island; Rhonda Morton of Airport Inn, Port Hardy; Nancy Dixon of Black Bear Resort; Karen Stewart of At Water's Edge B & B; Rick Salewski of Greyhound Canada, Victoria; Ali Macaraeg of Via Rail Canada Inc.; and Marie Ostrom of Marie's Bed and Breakfast, Bamfield.

I would also like to thank the following individuals for modelling for me at various locations across Canada: Becky, Luke, Cole and Gary Parkinson on their hike to Mount Robson; Dwaine Kowalsky for cycling the Icefields Parkway; Celia Tauzin for cycling the Dempster Highway; Carmen Boudreau for Old Montreal by caleche; Joe and Eli Nasogaluak with sculptures at the Great Northern Arts Festival; Effie, Jemma Gruben and Belinda Lavalee for the Arctic Toe Dip; Jeannine Pilon for the diamond-cutting demonstration; Godfrey Parsons for the iceberg tour; and Howard Collins at Cape St. Mary's Ecological Reserve in Newfoundland.

A special thanks to Sean, the pilot, and Tom White, the controller, at the Gander Airport; Gert from Alpine Aviation in Whitehorse; John Little of Babin Air; Cyril Rodgers of Qualicum Flight Centre, and Jim Armstrong of the Helicopter Company in Toronto, who flew me safely to and from Gros Morne, Kluane Glacier, Icefields Parkway, Della Falls and the CN Tower, respectively.

I would also like to thank Claude Bouchard, Michel Laverdiere, and Jeff Sewell for additional photography.

Last but not least, thanks to my good friend, cook and confidant Jean Lepage, who travelled with me to the four corners of Canada, and to Noel Hudson, who has written such a fantastic text for this book.

PHOTO CREDITS

All photographs by George Fischer except as indicated for the following pages:

Claude Bouchard, 27, 173, 254, 255; Kevin Callan, 119, 202-203; Kingfisher Wilderness Adventures, 29; Crown Jewel Resort, 167; Noel Hudson, 60-61; Michel Laverdiere (lighthouse detail) 117; Gary McGuffin, 22-23; James Raffan, 34-36, 124-125, 268-271; Carole Ross (portage) 122; Jeff Sewell 120, (tracks) 122; Judy Sewell, (red canoe) 121; Donald Standfield, 216; Gillian Stead, 113, 212; Travel Alberta, 25-26, 98-99, 145-146; Saskatchewan Tourism, pages 69, 108, 151; West Edmonton Mall, 74-75. Shutterstock: Richard C. Bennett (Dall's sheep) 16; Domhnall Dods (tall ship) 45; kristian (piping plover) 48; Tyler Olsen (sunset) 48; (canola) Jostein Hauge 49; Rick Thornton (swan) 49; photobank.ch (lone musician) 61; Tim Zurowski (sandpiper) 62; Mike Rogal (white-tailed deer) 68; W. Shane Dougherty (prickly pear cactus) 68; CoverStock (moose) 71; Richard C. Bennett (beaver) 72; Howard Sandler (balloons in sky) 86, 88; MaxFX (bee balloons, heating balloon) 87, 89; Howard Sandler (balloon group) 89; V.J. Matthew (rock caves) 94; Warren E. Simpson (fox) 96; magmarcz (heron) 96; Ferenc Cegledi (prairie dog) 109; Scott Pehrson (burrowing owl) 109; Michael Thompson (pronghorn antelope) 109; Mike Cavaroc (caribou) 133; Mike Rogal (fireworks) 134; Hisom Silviu (Parliament buildings) 135; Gina Smith (man with flag) 135; Sally Scott (arbutus tree) 137; Peter Graham (islands, steep hill) 138; Bellajay (St. Martin's shoreline) 139; Andre Nantel (summer view) 144; Vladimir Eremin (boardwalk) 144; Jason Cheever (Indian Village) 146; Tim Zurowski (snowy owl) 149; Tony Campbell (sandhill crane) 150; Stephen McSweeny (muledeer) 151; AioK (gannets) 172; Jason Grower (lobster buoys) 207; Keith Levit (Churchill, bears) 208-209; N. Joy Neish (Viking belongings) 242; Keith Levit (harbour) 243; Simon Krzic (Icelandic horse) 243; Muriel Lasure (mountain goat) 255; Richard C. Bennett (Dall's sheep) 258; Andrew Park (Manitoba Legislature) 160; Mike Rogal (Royal Mint) 161; Melissa King (coin) 161; V.J. Matthew (dirt road, Green Gables) 266, 267; Andrew Jebasingh (interior) 267.

BIBLIOGRAPHY

BOOKS

Berton, Pierre. *The Klondike Quest: A Photographic Essay 1897-1899*. Boston Mills Press, 2005.

Biagi, Susan, and Keith Vaughan. *Touring the Cabot Trail*, 2nd ed. Formac, 2005.

Bramble, Linda, and Shari Darling. *Discovering Ontario's Wine Country*. Boston Mills Press, 1994.

Bramble, Linda. *Touring Niagara's Wine Country*. Lorimer, 2000.

Byers, Mary, and John de Visser. *Lake Simcoe and Lake Couchiching*. Boston Mills Press, 2003.

Callan, Kevin. *Killarney*. Boston Mills Press, 1990.

Callan, Kevin. *A Paddler's Guide to Algonquin Park*. Boston Mills Press, 2004.

Callan, Kevin. *A Paddler's Guide to Killarney and the French River*. Boston Mills Press, 2006.

Clancy, Michael and Anna. *A User's Guide to Saskatchewan Parks*. University of Regina Press, 2006.

Corbett, Ron, and Malak Karsh. *The Gatineau*. Boston Mills Press, 1994.

Fischer, George, and Anthony Mollica. *Castles and Cottages: River Retreats of the Thousand Islands*. Boston Mills Press, 2004.

Fleming, Patricia, and John de Visser. *Thousand Islands*. Boston Mills Press, 1990.

Fodor's Nova Scotia and Atlantic Canada, 9th ed.: with New Brunswick, Prince Edward Island, and Newfoundland & Labrador. Fodor's, 2006.

Frommers and Bill McRae. *Frommer's British Columbia and the Canadian Rockies*, 4th ed. John Wiley & Sons Canada, Ltd., 2006.

Frommers and Paul Karr. *Frommer's Nova Scotia, New Brunswick and Prince Edward Island*, 6th ed. John Wiley & Sons Canada, Ltd. 2006.

Gill, Ian. *Haida Gwaii: Journeys Through the Queen Charlotte Islands*, 2nd rev. ed. Raincoast Books, 2004.

Gill, Ian. *Hiking on the Edge: The West Coast Trail and the Juan de Fuca Trail*, 3rd ed. Raincoast Books, 2002.

Holt, John. *Arctic Aurora: Canada's Yukon and Northwest Territories*. Nimbus Publishing, 2004.

James, Terry. *Buildings of Old Lunenburg*. Nimbus Publishing, 1996.

Kimantas, John. *The Wild Coast: A Kayaking, Hiking and Recreational Guide for North and West Vancouver Island*. Whitecap Books, 2005.

Legasse, Paul, ed. *The Columbia Concise Encyclopedia*, 3rd ed. Houghton Mifflin/Columbia University Press, 1995.

MacKay, Roderick, and William Reynolds. *Algonquin*. Boston Mills Press, 1995.

Maryniak, Barbara. *A Hiking Guide to the National Parks and Historic Sites of Newfoundland*. Goose Lane Editions, 1994.

McBurney, Marg, Mary Byers and John de Visser. *True Newfoundlanders: Early Homes and Families of Newfoundland and Labrador*. Boston Mills Press, 1997.

McGuffin, Gary, and Joanie McGuffin. *Superior: Journeys on an Inland Sea*. Boston Mills Press, 1995.

McGuffin, Gary, and Joanie McGuffin. *Wilderness Ontario*. Boston Mills Press, 2007.

Mueller, Marge, and Ted Mueller. *British Columbia's Gulf Islands*. Mountaineer Books, 2000.

Pole, Graeme. *Classic Hikes in the Canadian Rockies*, 2nd ed. Altitude Publishing, 2003.

Quinn, Eilis. *Montreal and Quebec City*. Lonely Planet, 2007

Raffan, James, ed. *Rendezvous with the Wild: The Boreal Forest*. Boston Mills Press, 2004.

Rand McNally Road Atlas: U.S./Canada/Mexico. Rand McNally & Company, 2006.

Reid, Gordon. *Dinosaur Provincial Park*. Boston Mills Press, 1986.

Reid, Gordon. *Head-Smashed-In Buffalo Jump*. Boston Mills Press, 1992.

Runtz, Michael. *The Howls of August: Encounters with Algonquin Wolves*. Boston Mills Press, 1997.

Runtz, Michael. *The Explorer's Guide to Algonquin Park*. Boston Mills Press, 2000.

Rogers, Barbara Radcliffe, and Stillman Rogers. *Canada's Atlantic Provinces: New Brunswick, Nova Scotia, Newfoundland, Prince Edward Island, Iles de La Madeleine, Labrador*, 3rd ed. Hunter Publishing, 2005.

Smith, Susan Weston. *The First Summer People: The Thousand Islands 1650-1910*. Boston Mills Press, 1993.

Western Arctic Handbook Committee. *Canada's Western Arctic: Including the Dempster Highway*. Gordon Soules Book Publishers, 2002.

Zimmerman, Karla, and Celeste Brash. *Nova Scotia, New Brunswick and Prince Edward Island*. Lonely Planet, 2007.

WEBSITES

www.adventureplus.org
www.agawacanyon.com
www.agawacanyontourtrain.com
www.alberta.ca
www.alertbay.com
www.algonquinpark.on.ca
www.archives.cbc.ca
www.archives.cnn.com
www.athropolis.com
www.banfflakelouise.com
www.bayoffundytourism.com
www.bcpassport.com
www.bigthings.ca
www.bonjourquebec.com
www.brackendaleartgallery.com
www.brackendaleeagles.com
www.britishcolumbia.com
www.calgarystampede.com
www.canadacool.com
www.canadatrails.ca
www.canadianencyclopedia.ca
www.canadiangeographic.ca
www.city.whitehorse.yk.ca
www.cityofdawson.com

www.civilization.ca
www.cntower.ca
www.columbiaicefield.com
www.communityprofiles.mb.ca
www.confederationbridge.com
www.coronach.ca
www.culture.alberta.ca
www.deborahcarr.ca
www.env.gov.bc.ca
www.env.gov.nl.ca
www.expeterra.com
www.fairmont.com
www.freshairadventure.com
www.fundyshoreecotour.ns.ca
www.gnaf.org
www.gov.pe.ca
www.greatcanadianparks.com
www.greatcanadianplaces.com
www.greatcanadianrivers.com
www.head-smashed-in.com
www.histori.ca
www.ilesdelamadeleine.com
www.k12.nf.ca
www.killerwhalecentre.org

www.mapleleafadventures.com
www.mint.ca
www.nationalgeographic.com
www.new-brunswick.net
www.ns.ec.gc.ca
www.nwcoast.com
www.nytimes.com
www.ontariooutdoor.com
www.ontarioparks.com
www.ontariotravel.net
www.pacificrimpaddling.com
www.peakfinder.com
www.peakware.com
www.peggys-cove.com
www.pei.worldweb.com
www.rockies.com
www.rockymountaineer.com
www.routedesphares.qc.ca
www.saskparks.ca
www.saskschools.ca
www.sepaq.com
www.simpson-air.com
www.spectacularnwt.com
www.summitsofcanada.ca

www.thecanadianencyclopedia.com
www.theculturedtraveler.com
www.tourismeilesdelamadeleine.com
www.tourismnewbrunswick.ca
www.townofhudsonbay.com
www.trails.com
www.transcanadahighway.com
www.trektravel.com
www.tuk.ca
www.tyrrellmuseum.com
www.unesco.org
www.urbanhipster.com
www.vancouver.ca
www.vancouverisland.com
www.viarail.ca
www.ville.gatineau.qc.ca
www.ville.montreal.qc.ca
www.virtualsk.com
www.visitwhitehorse.com
www.waterfallswest.com
www.westvancouver.com
www.whalespuffinsicebergs.com
www.worldeventsguide.com

Dempster Highway, Yukon and Northwest Territories

Index of Destinations

Entry Island, Quebec

UNFORGETTABLE
CANADA

100 DESTINATIONS

Alberta AB

British Columbia BC

Manitoba MB

New Brunswick NB

Newfoundland & Labrador NL

Northwest Territories NT

Nova Scotia NS

Nunavut NT

Ontario ON

Prince Edward Island PE

Quebec QC

Saskatchewan SK

Yukon YT